CHAPLAIN'S PROFESSIONAL HANDBOOK

Dr. Maxwell Shimba

Shimba Publishing, LLC

Table of Contents

THE HISTORY OF CHAPLAINCY iv

INTRODUCTION 1

QUALIFICATION 3

CHAPTER ONE 4

THE CHAPLAINCY 4

CHAPTER TWO 19

COMMUNICATION 19

PRISON AND JAIL MINISTRY 29

QUALIFICATIONS AND PREPARATION 38

PREPARATION 46

RELATING TO INMATE 50

HOW TO AVOID BECOMING THE VICTIM OF A SET-UP 76

CONTACT WITH INMATES 81

MINISTERING TO INMATE FAMILIES 95

DRESS CODES IN PENAL SYSTEMS 103

POST PRISON MINISTRY 106

HEALTHCARE CHAPLAINS 126

THE HOSPICE CONCEPT 133

STAGES OF DYING 176

DEATH AND CULTURAL GENERALITIES 190

DRESS CODES IN HOSPITALS, NURSING HOMES, AND HOSPICES 201

NOTES 208

THE HISTORY OF CHAPLAINCY

The history of chaplaincy can be traced back to ancient times when religious leaders accompanied armies into battle to provide spiritual support and guidance. However, the formalization of chaplaincy as a profession date back to the Middle Ages. The term "chaplain" itself comes from the Latin word "cappellanus," which refers to a priest or clergyman who is responsible for the care of a chapel.

During the Middle Ages, knights would often have a chaplain accompany them on their military campaigns. Chaplains were responsible for providing spiritual guidance to soldiers, administering the sacraments, and performing funeral rites. They were also responsible for caring for the wounded and dying, and for burying the dead. Many of these early chaplains were monks who lived with the soldiers in the field.

As the military began to grow and become more organized, the role of the chaplain became more specialized. In the 16th century, the Protestant Reformation brought about significant changes in the role of the chaplain. With the spread of Protestantism, chaplains began to serve not just soldiers, but also sailors, prisoners, and hospital patients.

During the American Civil War, chaplains played a vital role in providing comfort and support to soldiers on both sides of the conflict. Many chaplains were killed in battle, and their sacrifice helped to establish the profession as a respected and necessary part of the military.

In the 20th century, chaplaincy expanded to other areas beyond the military. Chaplains began serving in hospitals, universities, and other institutions, providing spiritual and emotional support to those in need. During World War II, chaplains played a critical role in providing spiritual support to soldiers, sailors, and airmen. They provided counseling, administered sacraments, and performed funeral services.

After the war, chaplaincy continued to grow and evolve. The Korean and Vietnam Wars brought new challenges to chaplains, who found themselves ministering to soldiers in new and difficult environments. During the Gulf War, chaplains provided support to soldiers in the field and helped them cope with the trauma of combat.

Today, chaplains serve in a wide variety of settings, from hospitals and universities to prisons and corporations. They provide spiritual and emotional support to people of all faiths and backgrounds and work closely with other professionals, such as counselors and social workers, to provide comprehensive care.

In the military, chaplains continue to play a vital role in supporting soldiers and their families. They provide counseling and support to soldiers and their families during times of stress and crisis and help them cope with the trauma of combat. Chaplains also provide religious services and sacraments and perform funerals and memorials for fallen soldiers.

In hospitals, chaplains provide spiritual and emotional support to patients and their families. They work closely with doctors, nurses, and other medical professionals to ensure that patients receive the best possible care. Chaplains also help patients cope with the emotional and spiritual aspects of illness and recovery.

In universities, chaplains provide support to students of all faiths and backgrounds. They help students navigate the challenges of college life and provide opportunities for spiritual growth and development. Chaplains also provide counseling and support to students during times of stress and crisis.

In prisons, chaplains provide spiritual support to inmates and help them prepare for reentry into society. They work closely with correctional officers and other prison staff to ensure that inmates receive the support they need to turn their lives around.

Chaplains are also increasingly being employed in the corporate world, where they provide support to employees facing workplace stress and other challenges. They help employees maintain a healthy work-life balance and provide opportunities for spiritual growth and development.

In the Christian tradition, chaplaincy began to take on a more formalized role during the Middle Ages when knights would often have a chaplain accompany them on their military campaigns. Chaplains were also present in hospitals and other institutions where they provided spiritual and emotional support to those in need.

During the Protestant Reformation in the 16th century, chaplaincy began to take on a more diverse role, with ministers accompanying not just soldiers but also sailors, prisoners, and hospital patients. The role of the chaplain continued to evolve throughout the centuries, with chaplains now serving in a wide variety of settings, including the military, hospitals, universities, and prisons. Today, chaplains of various faiths continue to provide spiritual and emotional support to people in need, often working in partnership with other professionals in fields like counseling and social work.

Hence, the history of chaplaincy dates back to ancient times, but the formalization of the profession dates back to the Middle Ages. Chaplains have played a vital role in providing spiritual and emotional support to soldiers, sailors

DR. MAXWELL SHIMBA

INTRODUCTION

Chaplains are spiritual leaders who offer support and guidance to people in various settings, including hospitals, hospices, prisons, military bases, and other institutions. They serve people of all faiths and beliefs, providing spiritual care and counseling to those who are experiencing difficult and challenging times in their lives. The role of a chaplain is multifaceted and requires a deep understanding of the needs and concerns of those they serve.

One of the primary roles of a chaplain is to provide emotional and spiritual support to individuals and families in crisis. They offer a listening ear and a compassionate heart, helping patients and their loved ones find peace and comfort in the midst of difficult circumstances. They may offer prayer, meditation, or other spiritual practices to help people connect with their faith and find meaning and purpose in their lives.

Chaplains also provide religious services and perform sacraments, such as baptisms, weddings, and funerals. They may lead worship services, deliver sermons, or administer holy communion, depending on the needs of the community they serve. They work closely with other religious leaders and may collaborate on interfaith events and programs.

In addition to providing spiritual care and counseling, chaplains play an important role in promoting healing and wellness. They work with healthcare professionals to create a holistic approach to care, addressing the physical, emotional, and spiritual needs of patients. They may offer guidance on nutrition, exercise, stress reduction, and other areas that contribute to overall health and well-being.

Chaplains also serve as advocates for patients and their families, ensuring that their needs are met and their voices are heard. They work with healthcare providers to develop care plans that are sensitive to cultural and spiritual beliefs, and they may help patients navigate the healthcare system to access the resources they need.

Another important role of chaplains is to support the staff and volunteers who work in healthcare and other institutions. They offer counseling, debriefing, and emotional support to those who may be struggling with the emotional toll of caring for others. They also provide training and education on topics such as cultural sensitivity, end-of-life care, and grief and loss.

Chaplains may work in a variety of settings, from hospitals and hospices to prisons and military bases. They may also serve as first responders in times of crisis, offering support and guidance to those affected by natural disasters, mass shootings, or other traumatic events.

Overall, the role of a chaplain is to provide spiritual care and support to individuals and families in need. They offer a compassionate presence and a listening ear, helping people find hope, healing, and peace in the midst of difficult circumstances. Their work is vital to the well-being of those they serve, and their impact is felt not only by individuals, but also by the communities and institutions they serve.

QUALIFICATION

The education and training requirements for chaplains vary depending on the type of chaplaincy and the institution or organization that employs them. Some chaplains may only require a high school diploma and specialized training in their field, while others may need advanced degrees and certification.

In general, chaplains working in healthcare settings such as hospitals or hospices are typically required to have at least a bachelor's degree, preferably in theology, religious studies, or a related field. Some institutions may require a master's degree or higher, as well as certification from a recognized chaplaincy organization.

Chaplains working in the military, correctional facilities, or other government agencies may also be required to have specific educational and training requirements, including completion of a chaplaincy program through the respective organization.

It is also important to note that chaplains are often required to have specialized training in areas such as counseling, crisis intervention, and ethics. Many chaplaincy programs include coursework and training in these areas to prepare chaplains for the unique challenges they may face in their role.

Hence, while a degree is not always required to become a chaplain, it is recommended and often required by institutions and organizations that employ chaplains. Additionally, specialized training and certification are typically required to ensure that chaplains have the necessary skills and knowledge to effectively serve their communities.

CHAPTER ONE

THE CHAPLAINCY

What is Chaplaincy?

A chaplaincy is a form of spiritual care that is provided by a chaplain, who is usually a religious leader or clergy member. Chaplains are trained to offer emotional and spiritual support to people who are experiencing difficult or traumatic situations, such as illness, injury, bereavement, or incarceration. They may work in a variety of settings, including hospitals, hospices, prisons, military bases, and universities, among others. The role of a chaplain is to provide a compassionate and non-judgmental presence, to listen and offer guidance, and to facilitate connections with religious or spiritual resources as desired by the individual. While chaplains are often affiliated with a specific religious tradition, they typically serve people of all faiths and beliefs, and may also work with those who are not religious.

The chaplains minister not to a congregation, but to the public at-large where the minister serves not in a church building nor "para-church" ministry, in contrast, in an institutional setting.

Example: Individuals who disclose themselves with a religion, it is customary to attend religious services. To these folks, attending services at temples, churches or other religious structures is often a very tectonic consequential part of their religious belief. Occasionally, however, members of a religion may not be able to attend services in their normal place of worship. It is during these times and occasions that they may have to rely on the services of a Chaplain.

The people who make up this Chaplaincy community may wear military uniforms, hospital gowns, hard hats, badges, and inmate orange-glow jumpsuits. Like the Apostle Paul, chaplains are generally "tent-makers": they usually have institutional administrative and staff jobs in addition to their ministries. But that is acceptable to chaplains, for serving in such "non-ministry" roles puts them in places where people – people with needs who ordinarily would never darken the doors of a church (much less talk to a minister) – come to talk and interact with the chaplain. The chaplain is there to listen, care, and respond appropriately to the agenda of the client. Such is the ministry of chaplaincy.

Services of a Chaplain

There are numerous types of chaplaincies. The following is a brief description of some of the more common chaplaincies and their requirements.

The services of a chaplain may vary depending on the setting in which they work, but generally, their primary role is to offer spiritual care and support to individuals and groups. Some of the common services provided by chaplains include:

1. Spiritual counseling and guidance: Chaplains provide a listening ear and offer guidance on spiritual matters to people who are facing challenging situations or experiencing personal crises.

2. Religious services: In some settings, chaplains may lead religious services or ceremonies, such as prayers, blessings, or funerals.
3. Emotional support: Chaplains offer emotional support to individuals and families during difficult times, such as illness, bereavement, or separation from loved ones.
4. Advocacy and referral: Chaplains may advocate on behalf of individuals and help connect them with appropriate resources or services, such as counseling, financial assistance, or legal aid.
5. Education and training: Chaplains may provide education and training to staff and volunteers on issues related to spiritual care, diversity, and cultural sensitivity.
6. Community building: Chaplains may work to foster a sense of community and belonging among individuals in their care, providing opportunities for prayer, meditation, or other spiritual practices.
7. Crisis intervention: In emergency situations, chaplains may provide crisis intervention and emotional support to first responders and those affected by the crisis.

Overall, the services of a chaplain are intended to provide emotional and spiritual support, and to help individuals and communities navigate difficult situations with compassion and care.

In brief: The services of a Chaplin are usually needed by those who are

- Correctional – Prison
- Homebound
- Healthcare
- In Hospice or Palliative Care
- In Nursing Homes
- Social Justices
- Military

➢ Workplace
➢ Educational
➢ Professional Counseling

Who is a Chaplain?

A chaplain is a person who provides spiritual care and support to individuals and groups in various settings such as hospitals, hospices, military, prisons, universities, and more. Chaplains may be ordained members of the clergy, but they can also be laypeople who are trained and authorized to provide spiritual care.

Chaplains are typically affiliated with a particular religious tradition, but they serve people of all faiths and beliefs, as well as those who do not identify with any particular religion. They offer emotional and spiritual support to individuals and families facing difficult situations, such as illness, death, or trauma, and may provide counseling, prayer, or other spiritual practices as appropriate.

Chaplains also work to build relationships with the communities they serve, providing education and training on issues related to spirituality, cultural sensitivity, and diversity. They may collaborate with other healthcare professionals or service providers to ensure that individuals receive the support and resources they need. Overall, chaplains play a critical role in supporting the spiritual and emotional well-being of individuals and communities.

A chaplain is essentially a spiritual representative attached to a secular institution. Chaplains may or may not be certified, have a theological education, or be ordained or commissioned by a particular denomination, though many are. While chaplaincy has traditionally been associated with representatives of the Christian faith, the term is now used for representatives of any faith. Some chaplains are expected to represent multiple faiths, acting as a sort of neutral spiritual resource.

A Chaplain offers spiritual care to individuals outside of a church context. As a Volunteer Chaplain, you will be expected to minister to those who have different religious, spiritual and cultural backgrounds. As a chaplain, your main tasks will involve listening, comforting and praying with people who need spiritual support in difficult situations. Remember, listen, comfort, pray, and support.

As a Chaplain you must be all things to all people without compromising your own faith, at the same time respecting the faith of others. Being a Chaplain is not being a pastor or priest or some religious leader, but a servant to all people regardless of what your faith maybe. A chaplain must have the heart of a volunteer.

Military. Young people preparing for and going to war need pastoral care! There are Active Duty, Reserves, National Guard chaplains in the Army, Air Force, Navy, Marines, and Coast Guard. Requirements are a Bachelor's degree and a Master of Divinity degree, usually earned before the fortieth birthday. The Air Force and Navy also sponsor volunteer chaplaincy in the Civil Air Patrol and Sea Cadet programs, respectively.

A Note of Concern in November 2014. There seems to be some confusion of roles, responsibilities, and opportunities within the military chaplaincy. Some endorsing bodies seem to think that producing chaplains is a "right" of their faith group and, more troubling, that chaplains have the "right" [and perhaps God-mandated requirement] to attempt to evangelize and proselytize military personnel and their families as they see fit. That was not what I believe the Founding Fathers intended when they established chaplaincy in the military in 1775. And as our nation becomes increasingly religiously and philosophically more diverse, so does our nation's military. Today's chaplains who serve our military must be acutely aware of their responsibilities — and potential impact – within this unique context for ministry and influence.

In Huffington Post (see Religious Accommodation — A Wolf in Sheep's Clothing) an endorser has written:

"Military chaplains exist first and foremost "to perform or provide for the free exercise of religion." There is a sacred institutional trust that chaplains must save their theology and creeds for formal worship services and/or private, client-invited pastoral counseling. Suicide prevention presentations and other mandatory presentations, ceremonies, and personnel formations are NOT the time to theologically opine and sermonize. Chaplains should and are mandated to be sensitive to the needs of A-L-L in their spiritual care and institutional responsibility — and they are never to attempt to proselytize or even opine when such possibly can be construed as either coercive or an undue influence! I would think that such actions in the context of mandatory formations and presentations and even written columns in official unit publications could easily be construed as command-sponsored or command-endorsed policies or positions and as such are likely violations of that sacred trust, if not outright illegal. If professional military chaplains are uncomfortable laboring with sensitivity and sincere adherence to and genuine respect for their proper roles in such contexts, it may be time for some chaplains to reconsider their sense of calling and definition of ministry — before the military is compelled to take action to insure the rights as well as the (career and emotional) safety of personnel."

I feel that this is really good and accurate — and a great quote to place here!!!!

Healthcare. Veterans' Affairs and civilian hospitals, as well as hospices, hire professional chaplains. Who better to reach the hopeless, hurting, and dying of society than caring well-trained chaplains? To be a healthcare chaplain generally requires a Bachelor's degree, a Master of Divinity degree or equivalent, and one year of clinical pastoral training in a healthcare context.

Correctional. God has seen to it that the felon has a chance to contemplate his/her crimes against society. Who better to reach out to the lost, hopeless, desperate, and forgotten of society with a message of deliverance, and hope than a dedicated chaplain? There are professional and volunteer opportunities in our nation's Federal, state, and local facilities. It is said that corrections are presently the fastest growing industry in America. Could the Lord be calling you to minister true freedom to those who have known nothing but bondage? Or, to support chaplains who do? Requirements vary according to the correctional facility; most require at least a Bachelor's degree. Volunteer positions are plentiful and do not require degrees.

Workplace. Business and industrial chaplaincy is a new and growing field. Employees not distracted by marriage and family crises, alcohol, drugs, and other addictions, as well as a myriad of personal and spiritual problems are safer, more productive employees. Studies indicate that for every dollar spent on workplace chaplaincy results in a $4 to $7 saving for business due to absenteeism, accidents, medical and counseling intervention and treatment, etc. Specializations in the field of workplace chaplaincy include union, truck stop, airport, seaport, fire department, police department, race track, and college chaplaincies. Requirements for these chaplaincies vary considerably.

Educational. Public School Chaplaincy for America™ is the only organization that equips clergy for ministry to students, faculty, and administrators in public schools in the US. A quick glance of the top tragedies of the last several years makes the mandate for this new genre of pastoral care painfully clear! Requirements are appropriate specialized training, criminal background check, and ecclesiastical endorsement.

Professional Counseling. While professional pastoral counseling is not chaplaincy, it is an endorsable ministry that desperately needs Spirit-filled representation. Professional counselors hold state licensure(s) and/or secular certification(s) as marriage and family therapists, alcohol and drug rehabilitation counselors, psychologists, etc. Requirements for professional counselors are generally a Bachelor's degree, a graduate degree in psychology or counseling, and a number of hours in a supervised counseling practicum. While these requisites may seem "stiff," think of the impact that pastoral counselors would have on the lives of those who has lost their way, as well as the people of faith who may need a little extra help in life!

THE DUTIES OF THE CHAPLAINCY

The duties of the chaplaincy can vary depending on the setting in which the chaplain works, but generally, chaplains have the following responsibilities:

1. Spiritual care: Chaplains provide spiritual care and support to individuals and groups, including prayer, counseling, and other spiritual practices.
2. Emotional support: Chaplains offer emotional support to individuals and families during difficult times, such as illness, death, or separation from loved ones.
3. Advocacy and referral: Chaplains may advocate on behalf of individuals and help connect them with appropriate resources or services, such as counseling, financial assistance, or legal aid.
4. Religious services: In some settings, chaplains may lead religious services or ceremonies, such as prayers, blessings, or funerals.
5. Education and training: Chaplains may provide education and training to staff and volunteers on issues related to spiritual care, diversity, and cultural sensitivity.
6. Community building: Chaplains may work to foster a sense of community and belonging among individuals in their care, providing opportunities for prayer, meditation, or other spiritual practices.
7. Crisis intervention: In emergency situations, chaplains may provide crisis intervention and emotional support to first responders and those affected by the crisis.
8. Confidentiality: Chaplains are required to maintain confidentiality with the information they receive from individuals in their care, except in situations where there is a risk of harm to themselves or others.

Accordingly, the duties of the chaplaincy are focused on providing emotional and spiritual support, promoting a sense of community and belonging, and advocating for the needs of individuals in their care.

What Does a Chaplain Do?

A chaplain is a spiritual caregiver who provides emotional and spiritual support to individuals and groups in a variety of settings, such as hospitals, hospices, military bases, prisons, and universities. Here are some of the things that a chaplain typically does:

1. Provides spiritual care: Chaplains offer spiritual care and support to individuals of all faiths and beliefs. This may include counseling, prayer, meditation, or other spiritual practices.
2. Offers emotional support: Chaplains provide emotional support to people who are experiencing difficult situations, such as illness, death, or trauma. They listen, offer comfort, and help people process their emotions.
3. Conducts religious services: In some settings, chaplains lead religious services or ceremonies, such as baptisms, weddings, or funerals.
4. Advocates for individuals: Chaplains may advocate on behalf of individuals and help them connect with resources or services, such as counseling, financial assistance, or legal aid.
5. Build relationships: Chaplains work to build relationships with the communities they serve, providing education and training on issues related to spirituality, cultural sensitivity, and diversity.
6. Provides crisis intervention: In emergency situations, chaplains may provide crisis intervention and emotional support to first responders and those affected by the crisis.
7. Maintains confidentiality: Chaplains are required to maintain confidentiality with the information they receive from individuals in their care, except in situations where there is a risk of harm to themselves or others.

Overall, the role of a chaplain is to provide compassionate and non-judgmental support to individuals and groups, helping them to navigate difficult situations with dignity and respect.

Chaplains led nondenominational religious services and provide spiritual support to those who are unable to attend organized religious services. A chaplain may work in a hospital, prison, or university, or serve as part of the military. Although prison, military, school, and hospital chaplains work in very different environments, they all provide spiritual guidance to individuals who don't have access to formal religious services offered by their faith of choice.

Note that: The work of the Chaplaincy differs from that of the Pastorate. Pastors care for the spiritual needs of the congregation whereas Chaplains must care for the needs of the secular world as well.

Chaplains are expected to serve the spiritual and emotional needs of others. Some chaplains perform wedding or funeral ceremonies, administer communion, deliver spiritual messages, offer prayer at public meetings, and provide regular counseling. Other chaplains meet the need of the moment, usually through listening and prayer. Chaplains may also function as advocates; hospital chaplains, for example, may make requests of a nurse to help meet a particular patient's needs; military chaplains may provide for marriage enrichment retreats.

Chaplains work in many environments. Most commonly, chaplains are attached to the military, to hospitals, to law enforcement and fire departments, to political bodies (such as the United States Congress and Senate), to sports teams, and to educational institutions. Some corporations, music groups, and even households (historically the nobility, and now certain monarchs), may also employ chaplains.

Furthermore, Chaplains offer a service of spiritual care to individuals from all walks of life. In order to be effective in the Chaplaincy, one must have the:

- ✓ Ability to build a rapport with others through effective listening skills
- ✓ Ability to communicate effectively
- ✓ Ability to work as a team member with staff
- ✓ Willingness to work with and meet the spiritual needs of people of all religious faiths, ages, genders, sexual orientations, cultures, and races.
- ✓ Ability to deal with stress and crisis

It is out of the integrity of their personal spirituality that Chaplains are sensitive to and supportive of the diverse spiritual and religious needs of the people they serve. As a Volunteer Chaplain, your services may also be requested by staff members. Increasingly, staff members have been turning to Chaplains for advice, support and, a pastoral relationship. Many people view Chaplains as friends who have the time to listen in absolute confidence. Chaplains are considered unique among the professional staff because their services primarily focus on religion and spirituality.

A chaplain's most important job is to provide religious services, spiritual guidance, and counseling to those in need. According to O-Net Online, a website created for the U.S. Department of Labor, a chaplain gives sermons to encourage spirituality and provide comfort.

A chaplain who works in a hospital or hospice facility provides counseling and spiritual guidance for patients, their families, and even the hospital staff. Chaplains may also provide educational programs or conversion counseling to youth or prisoners. Chaplains can perform religious rites such as weddings and funerals as well. Depending on their work environment, chaplains may plan and coordinate retreats and training for others who perform religious services and spiritual counseling.

Facts about Chaplains

Here are some facts about chaplains:

1. The word "chaplain" comes from the Latin word "cappellanus", which originally referred to a person who kept the cloak (cappa) of a bishop.
2. Chaplains serve in a variety of settings, including hospitals, hospices, military bases, prisons, universities, and more.
3. Chaplains may be ordained members of the clergy, but they can also be laypeople who are trained and authorized to provide spiritual care.
4. Chaplains serve people of all faiths and beliefs, as well as those who do not identify with any particular religion.
5. Chaplains are trained to provide emotional and spiritual support to individuals and families facing difficult situations, such as illness, death, or trauma.
6. Chaplains may provide counseling, prayer, meditation, or other spiritual practices as appropriate.
7. Chaplains may advocate on behalf of individuals and help them connect with appropriate resources or services.
8. Chaplains are required to maintain confidentiality with the information they receive from individuals in their care, except in situations where there is a risk of harm to themselves or others.
9. Chaplains work to build relationships with the communities they serve, providing education and training on issues related to spirituality, cultural sensitivity, and diversity.
10. Chaplains play a critical role in supporting the emotional and spiritual well-being of individuals and communities, and their services are often highly valued and appreciated.

A chaplain is typically a priest, pastor, ordained deacon or other member of the clergy. They usually serve a group of people who are not organized as a mission or church, or who are unable to attend church for many reasons, such as poor health, confinement, or military or civil duties.

Chaplains are representatives of their faith communities, simultaneously, require them to live out the commitment of those communities to the wider world. Chaplains must therefore be learned in the ways of the faith group and be intelligent and well informed about the basis for its decisions and guidance. In this position and or function, Chaplains are amenable and liable to the faith assemblage for embodying its ethics and teachings appropriately.

Chaplains have to deal with some of the most excruciating difficulty individuals personage experiences that result from illness and injury. They are often uniquely placed to relate to people in these circumstances, to discern their needs, and to provide forms of pastoral care. Chaplains also nurture well-being, foster hope and support people through the transitional periods of life.

One important facet of the Chaplain's purpose and function is in the ability to simultaneously represent spiritual and the religious embodiment of faith for other people. Such an externalization leads the spectator to project on the Chaplain their views and expectations. They may be simple or convoluted, confused or clear, placid or angry. Without compromising their integrity, Chaplains expected to express the spiritual needs of someone in a meaningful and relevant way.

The spiritual dimension of life expresses purpose and meaning. The spiritual dimension evokes feelings which demonstrate love, faith, hope, trust, awe and inspirations; therein providing meaning and a reason for existence. It comes into focus particularly when a person faces stress, illness or death. Chaplains must be spiritually sensitive to the needs of those they service.

Notwithstanding, it is misapprehension to think that people solely talk of religious matters to Chaplains and correspondingly a mistake to think that these are the exclusively matters that Chaplains are interested in or concerned about. Chaplains are concerned in all aspects of life and care of the persons they service.

CHAPTER TWO

COMMUNICATION

Communication is defined as a process by which information is exchanged between individuals through a common system of symbols, signs, or behavior.

Accordingly, effective communication is an essential skill for chaplains, who must be able to connect with individuals and groups from diverse backgrounds and help them navigate difficult emotional and spiritual situations. Here are some principles of effective communication in chaplaincy:

1. Active listening: Chaplains must be skilled in active listening, which involves paying close attention to what individuals are saying, asking clarifying questions, and providing empathetic responses.
2. Cultural competence: Chaplains should have an understanding of different cultural, religious, and spiritual traditions and be able to communicate effectively with people from diverse backgrounds.
3. Non-judgmental attitude: Chaplains must be able to approach individuals and situations without judgment or bias, creating a safe and welcoming space for people to share their thoughts and feelings.

4. Empathy: Chaplains should be able to put themselves in the shoes of the people they serve, demonstrating empathy and understanding for their struggles and concerns.
5. Clarity: Chaplains must be able to communicate their thoughts and ideas clearly and concisely, using language that is appropriate and understandable for the individuals they serve.
6. Respect: Chaplains should always treat the individuals they serve with respect and dignity, acknowledging their beliefs and experiences.
7. Confidentiality: Chaplains must be able to maintain confidentiality with the information they receive from individuals in their care, creating an atmosphere of trust and safety.

Thus, the art of communication in chaplaincy involves being able to connect with individuals and groups from diverse backgrounds in a respectful, empathetic, and non-judgmental manner, creating a safe and welcoming space for people to share their thoughts and feelings.

Rules of Communication

While there is no one-size-fits-all set of rules for communication in chaplaincy, there are some general principles that chaplains can follow to enhance their effectiveness as communicators. Here are some rules of communication that may be helpful for chaplains:

1. Listen actively: Focus on the speaker and give them your full attention. Listen for both content and emotion, and ask open-ended questions to encourage further dialogue.
2. Respect differences: Recognize and respect cultural, religious, and spiritual differences. Don't impose your own

beliefs or values on others, but instead seek to understand their perspective.

3. Use appropriate language: Use language that is respectful, inclusive, and culturally sensitive. Avoid using jargon or technical terms that may be confusing or offensive.

4. Be empathetic: Try to understand the other person's perspective, feelings, and experiences. Show empathy and support, and avoid criticizing or judging.

5. Speak clearly and concisely: Use simple and clear language, avoiding jargon or overly complex terminology. Be concise and to the point, while still being respectful and compassionate.

6. Maintain confidentiality: Respect the privacy of the person you are communicating with. Keep any information shared with you confidential, unless there is a risk of harm to yourself or others.

7. Follow up: If appropriate, follow up with the person after the communication to check on their progress or offer further support.

By following these rules of communication, chaplains can enhance their ability to connect with people from diverse backgrounds, provide emotional and spiritual support, and create an atmosphere of trust and safety.

- ✓ Learn to Listen
- ✓ Be open and honest
- ✓ Be tactful, considerate, and courteous
- ✓ Be clear and specific
- ✓ Be realistic and reasonable
- ✓ Be polite and courteous
- ✓ Be patient and understanding
- ✓ Speak softly
- ✓ Be consistent and sincere
- ✓ Be friendly and smile

✓   Do not preach or lecture

✓   Do not excuse or fall for excuses

✓   Recognize that each event can be seen from different points of view

✓   Do not allow discussion to turn into destructive arguments

✓   Let effectiveness, not intention, be the goal of your communications

✓   Accept all feelings and try to be understanding of them

✓   Know when to use humor and when to be serious

Following the rules of communication ensures the building of positive rapport. Positive rapport is marked by harmony, conformity, accord or affinity in a relationship. The key to building rapport is communication. Communication begins with good listening skills.

The Power of Good Listening Skills

The power of good listening skills should never be underestimated. Good listening skills help Chaplains to provide excellent service. When a person listen's properly, it assures the speaker that their issues are important to the listener. Good listening skills however are not natural for human beings. Our brain was made to multitask and is easily distracted. Therefore, in order to be a good listener, discipline is needed because there is a big difference between Hearing and Listening.

Wherefore, good listening skills are critical for chaplains, who often work with people who are facing difficult emotional and spiritual situations. Here are some reasons why good listening skills are important for chaplains:

1. Builds trust: When people feel listened to, they are more likely to trust the person who is listening. By being a good listener, chaplains can build trust with the individuals they serve, creating a safe and supportive environment.
2. Demonstrates empathy: Good listening skills demonstrate empathy and compassion for the individuals who are sharing their stories. This can help chaplains better understand their needs and concerns and provide more effective support.
3. Promotes self-reflection: By actively listening to others, chaplains can help individuals gain insight into their own thoughts and feelings, leading to greater self-awareness and personal growth.
4. Encourages dialogue: Good listening skills encourage open and honest dialogue, allowing individuals to express their thoughts and feelings without fear of judgment or criticism.
5. Enhances problem-solving: By listening carefully to individuals' concerns, chaplains can help them identify and address specific challenges they may be facing, leading to more effective problem-solving.
6. Creates a sense of connection: Good listening skills create a sense of connection and community, fostering a supportive environment where individuals can share their stories and experiences with others.

Therefore, good listening skills are essential for chaplains, as they help build trust, demonstrate empathy, promote self-reflection, encourage dialogue, enhance problem-solving, and create a sense of connection. By listening carefully and attentively to the individuals they serve, chaplains can provide effective emotional and spiritual support and make a positive difference in people's lives.

> The words we speak are very powerful and true listening is a manifestation of love.

The power of our words cannot be underestimated. The things we say can have a profound impact on those around us, shaping their perceptions of themselves and the world around them. Words can be used to uplift, inspire, and encourage, but they can also be used to hurt, demean, and tear down.

True listening, on the other hand, is a manifestation of love. When we truly listen to someone, we are showing them that we value them and their thoughts and feelings. We are giving them our full attention and allowing them to express themselves without judgment or interruption. This can be incredibly healing and empowering for the person speaking, as they feel seen, heard, and validated.

Unfortunately, in our fast-paced and often distracted world, true listening is becoming increasingly rare. Many people are more focused on getting their own point across or checking their phones than on truly engaging with the person in front of them. This can leave others feeling lonely, disconnected, and unimportant.

But when we make a conscious effort to truly listen to others, we can create deep and meaningful connections with them. We can learn from their experiences and perspectives, and we can help them feel supported and understood. We can also model the kind of listening we would like to receive, creating a ripple effect of kindness and compassion.

In conclusion, the words we speak are powerful, and we should use them wisely and with intention. True listening, on the other hand, is a manifestation of love and can help us build deeper connections with those around us. By valuing and respecting the thoughts and feelings of others, we can create a more empathetic and compassionate world.

Question:

When a person responds to your words by saying "I hear you," do you sometimes wonder if they were truly listening to you? Perhaps you find your mind wandering off when someone is sharing her thoughts with you. You may have heard the words being spoken, but were you really listening to their meaning?

Hearing and listening have quite different meanings. Hearing is a passive occurrence that requires no effort. Listening, on the other hand, is a conscious choice that demands your attention and concentration.

It is possible that a person who says "I hear you" may not have truly been listening to what was said. The phrase "I hear you" is often used as a polite acknowledgement of the other person's words, without necessarily indicating a deeper understanding or engagement with the content of the message.

Truly listening to someone involves not just hearing their words, but also actively engaging with what they are saying, seeking to understand their perspective and feelings, and demonstrating empathy and respect. It requires focusing your attention on the person speaking, and setting aside distractions or preconceived notions that might interfere with understanding.

It is important to remember that effective communication is a two-way process that involves both speaking and listening. When we communicate, we should strive to be both clear in our own expression and receptive to the perspectives of others.

Exploring Various Levels of Listening

LISTENING IN SPURTS

Listening in spurts is a common habit that some people have. It means that they are only partially paying attention to what is being said and may be distracted by other thoughts or stimuli. This type of listening can lead to misunderstandings and miscommunications, as important information may be missed or misinterpreted. It is important to practice active listening, which involves fully engaging with the speaker and giving them your full attention, in order to promote effective communication and understanding.

QUIET/PASSIVE LISTENING

Quiet/passive listening is a type of listening where the listener is physically present and not interrupting, but not actively engaged in the conversation. They may appear to be listening, nodding their head, and making eye contact, but they are not fully engaged in the conversation. This type of listening often leads to misunderstandings and miscommunications as important details may be missed. The quiet/passive listener may also miss nonverbal cues and body language that would provide additional context and meaning to the conversation. It is important for the listener to actively engage in the conversation by asking questions and clarifying points to ensure full understanding.

ACTIVE LISTENING

Active listening is a communication skill that involves fully focusing on and comprehending what the speaker is saying, as well as observing their body language and tone of voice to understand the underlying emotions and thoughts.

The key attributes of active listening include:

1. Paying attention: The listener gives their full attention to the speaker, avoiding distractions and external interruptions.
2. Responding appropriately: The listener uses verbal and nonverbal cues to show they are engaged and listening, such as nodding, making eye contact, and providing feedback or clarifying questions.
3. Withholding judgment: The listener avoids jumping to conclusions or making assumptions about the speaker's motives or intentions, and instead seeks to understand their perspective without judgment.
4. Reflecting and paraphrasing: The listener reflects back what the speaker has said, using their own words to ensure they

have understood correctly and to show empathy and understanding.

5. Summarizing and clarifying: The listener summarizes and clarifies what has been said to ensure they have a complete understanding of the speaker's thoughts and feelings.

Active listening is a fundamental skill for chaplains and other caregivers who work closely with people in emotional distress or facing challenging situations. By fully listening to and understanding their patients' concerns, chaplains can better provide emotional and spiritual support that addresses their specific needs. Active listening helps chaplains build trust with patients and create a safe space for them to share their thoughts and feelings.

IMPAIRMENTS TO LISTENING

There are several impairments that can affect a person's ability to listen effectively. Some of them are:

1. Physical Impairments: These include hearing loss or impairment, which can make it difficult to hear what others are saying. In such cases, the listener may need to use assistive devices such as hearing aids to enhance their listening abilities.

2. Mental Impairments: Mental impairments like attention deficit hyperactivity disorder (ADHD) or other mental health conditions can make it difficult for a person to concentrate and focus on what others are saying.

3. Emotional Distractions: Emotional distractions like stress, anxiety, or depression can impact a person's ability to listen actively. It can lead to a lack of concentration or result in the person being preoccupied with their own thoughts and feelings.

4. Cultural Differences: Cultural differences can create barriers to effective listening. A person's communication style, use of language, and nonverbal cues may be different from others.

These differences can lead to misunderstandings and misinterpretations.

5. Environmental Factors: Environmental factors like background noise or poor lighting can make it difficult to hear or understand what is being said.

6. Personal Bias: Personal bias can also impact a person's ability to listen effectively. If a person has preconceived notions or judgments about the speaker, it can influence how they interpret the message.

It is important to be aware of these impairments and work on overcoming them to improve our listening skills.

- ✘ Fatigue
- ✘ Hunger
- ✘ Dehydration
- ✘ Illness
- ✘ Cell Phones
- ✘ Texting

PRISON AND JAIL MINISTRY

Prison Ministry has a direct Scriptural Mandate (Matthew 25:31-40). Throughout the Bible are examples, descriptions, and commandments about prisons, prisoners, bondage, captivity, and slavery. The Bible mentions prison, prisoners, or imprisonment more than 130 times. We should follow the example Christ set by ministering to prisoners. Prisoners meet the criteria of any mission field: Lost people and a need for laborers.

Prison and jail ministry involves providing emotional and spiritual support to incarcerated individuals, as well as to their families and loved ones. The goal of this ministry is to help individuals in prison or jail find hope, healing, and a sense of purpose, regardless of their past mistakes or current circumstances. Here are some key aspects of prison and jail ministry:

1. Outreach: Prison and jail ministry often involves reaching out to incarcerated individuals through letters, phone calls, or in-person visits. Chaplains or volunteers may provide pastoral care, counseling, or other forms of emotional and spiritual support to inmates.
2. Worship services: Many prisons and jails offer religious services, and chaplains or volunteers may lead or participate in these services. These services can provide a sense of community and support to incarcerated individuals.
3. Bible study and discipleship: Chaplains or volunteers may also lead Bible study or discipleship groups in prisons and

jails, helping individuals grow in their faith and develop a deeper understanding of spiritual principles.

4. Re-entry support: As individuals prepare to re-enter society after their release from prison or jail, prison and jail ministry may involve providing support for their transition. This may include job training, counseling, or other resources to help individuals successfully reintegrate into their communities.

5. Family support: Prison and jail ministry may also involve providing emotional and spiritual support to the families and loved ones of incarcerated individuals. This can include counseling, prayer support, and other forms of assistance to help them cope with the challenges of having a loved one in prison or jail.

Hence, prison and jail ministry play an important role in helping incarcerated individuals find hope, healing, and a sense of purpose, as well as supporting their families and loved ones. By providing emotional and spiritual support, prison and jail ministry can help individuals transform their lives and overcome the challenges of incarceration.

Chaplains on staff at a prison cannot minister to more than a small percentage of inmates in their care. They cannot do all of the necessary work themselves, as there is just not enough time to do so. For every person incarcerated, there are three to five other people affected: mates, children, parents, etc. Inmate and their families represent a large segment of society in any culture. As a Volunteer Chaplain, you may have to service those affected by the incarceration as well as the person who is incarcerated.

Spiritual Goals of jail and Prison Ministry

The spiritual goals of jail and prison ministry are to provide incarcerated individuals with the opportunity to grow in their faith, deepen their relationship with God, and find hope, healing, and a sense of purpose. Here are some key spiritual goals of jail and prison ministry:

1. Encourage repentance: One of the primary spiritual goals of jail and prison ministry is to encourage incarcerated individuals to recognize their mistakes and turn their lives over to God. Chaplains or volunteers may provide counseling, prayer support, and other forms of spiritual guidance to help individuals take responsibility for their actions and seek forgiveness.

2. Foster spiritual growth: Jail and prison ministry also seeks to help incarcerated individuals grow in their faith and develop a deeper relationship with God. This may involve leading Bible study or discipleship groups, providing pastoral care, or offering other forms of spiritual support.

3. Promote forgiveness: Another important spiritual goal of jail and prison ministry is to promote forgiveness, both for oneself and for others. By helping individuals understand the power of forgiveness, chaplains or volunteers can help them find inner peace and healing.

4. Provide hope: Jail and prison ministry seeks to provide hope to incarcerated individuals, reminding them that they are valued by God and that they have the potential to lead fulfilling lives, even in the midst of difficult circumstances.

5. Support reintegration: Finally, jail and prison ministry aim to support incarcerated individuals in their efforts to successfully reintegrate into their communities after their release. This may involve providing job training, counseling, or other resources to help them build a new life outside of prison or jail.

Overall, the spiritual goals of jail and prison ministry are to help incarcerated individuals find hope, healing, and a deeper relationship with God, as well as to support their efforts to make positive changes in their lives and successfully reintegrate into their communities.

The spiritual goals of jail and prison ministry may include one or more of the following:

- ✓ To share the unconditional love of God
- ✓ To disciple new believers in the Word and teach them how to study the Holy Scriptures
- ✓ To demonstrate the Power of Prayer and teach them how to pray
- ✓ To lead inmates to experience the life-changing power of God that will free them from guilt, shame, negative emotions and addictions
- ✓ To minister to inmates' families if feasible or practical

Social goals of Jail and Prison Ministry

In addition to spiritual goals, jail and prison ministry also has important social goals. These goals focus on helping incarcerated individuals to develop positive social relationships, to develop life skills, and to become productive members of society after their release from prison or jail. Here are some key social goals of jail and prison ministry:

1. Address social issues: Jail and prison ministry seeks to address the social issues that contribute to criminal behavior, such as poverty, addiction, and lack of education. Chaplains or volunteers may provide counseling, resources, and other forms of support to help individuals overcome these issues and make positive changes in their lives.

2. Encourage community building: Jail and prison ministry may also involve building community within prisons and jails, providing a sense of belonging and support to incarcerated individuals. This can help reduce tensions and conflicts

within the prison or jail environment and foster positive social relationships among inmates.

3. Provide life skills training: Another important social goal of jail and prison ministry is to provide life skills training, such as job training, financial management, and conflict resolution. This can help incarcerated individuals to develop the skills they need to succeed after their release from prison or jail.

4. Support reentry: Jail and prison ministry also aims to support individuals as they prepare to re-enter society after their release. This may involve providing resources, counseling, and other forms of support to help them successfully reintegrate into their communities.

5. Advocate for criminal justice reform: Finally, jail and prison ministry may also involve advocating for criminal justice reform, addressing issues such as overcrowding, inadequate healthcare, and inadequate resources for reentry. By advocating for these changes, jail and prison ministry can help create a more just and equitable criminal justice system.

Overall, the social goals of jail and prison ministry are to help incarcerated individuals develop positive social relationships, acquire life skills, and become productive members of society after their release. By addressing social issues, building community, providing life skills training, and supporting reentry, jail and prison ministry can help reduce recidivism and promote positive change.

- ✓ To help inmates function more positively within the prison environment
- ✓ To provide a bridge between the community and individuals confined in correctional facilities
- ✓ To prepare residents for reentry into society (physically, mentally, morally and spiritually)
- ✓ To assist inmates' families in practical ways
- ✓ To provide post-prison assistance in practical ways

WHAT IS YOUR ROLE?

There are millions of active believers worldwide, but only a small number are involved in ministry to prisoners despite the fact that jails and prisons are found in almost every community. The scriptural mandate by both teaching and example is clear; this is not to say that you are called to go into the prison. As in any missions, everyone is not called to go into a foreign field to share the Gospel. But as in missions, every believer should be involved in prison ministry in some capacity.

It is important for you, as a Volunteer Chaplain, to have some understanding of Jail and Prison Chaplains. Prison Chaplains work long hours under difficult conditions. Each day Chaplains on staff must deal with many responsibilities such as the personal crises of inmates, providing programs to meet the spiritual needs of inmates, and fighting the frustrations and disappointments which are an integral part of Prison Chaplaincy.

Prison Chaplains must also be acceptable to the warden of the prison in which they are to work. The Prison Chaplain functions as the administrator of a religious program for the entire institution. The Staff Chaplain for the institution provides traditional teaching, oversees religious education programs; spends much time in personal counseling; and recruits, trains and supervises Volunteer Chaplains. They also perform various administrative activities such as managing correspondence, conducting meetings and completing reports.

It is important for the Volunteer Chaplain to maintain a good relationship with the Chaplain on staff. It is a grave breach of trust to use your access to the prison to undermine the Chaplains' reputation or to discredit his program. If there is a problem, always talk to the Chaplain first.

WAYS TO BE INVOLVED

There are many reasons to be involved in prison ministry. Here are some of the most common reasons:

1. Help others: The prison ministry offers a unique opportunity to make a positive impact on the lives of incarcerated individuals. By providing spiritual and emotional support, mentoring, and other forms of assistance, you can help individuals who may be feeling isolated, hopeless, and disconnected from society.

2. Fulfill a calling: Many people feel called to prison ministry as a way to serve God and make a difference in the world. If you feel a strong sense of purpose or calling to this type of work, getting involved in prison ministry may be a way to live out your faith and serve others.

3. Gain new perspectives: Working in prison ministry can also provide an opportunity to gain new perspectives on the criminal justice system, social issues, and the human experience. Through your interactions with incarcerated individuals, you may gain insights into the root causes of crime and the challenges faced by individuals who are impacted by the criminal justice system.

4. Build relationships: Prison ministry can be a great way to build meaningful relationships with individuals who may have different backgrounds and life experiences from your own. Through these relationships, you may learn new things, gain a deeper understanding of the human experience, and develop a greater appreciation for the diversity of humanity.

5. Make a difference in your community: By supporting individuals in prison, you can also make a difference in your community as a whole. By helping individuals successfully

reintegrate into society after their release, you can help reduce recidivism and promote positive change in your community. Accordingly, getting involved in prison ministry can be a deeply rewarding experience that offers an opportunity to make a positive impact on the lives of incarcerated individuals, gain new perspectives, build relationships, and make a difference in your community.

Note the following:

- ✓ Provide prayer and support for prison ministries
- ✓ Visit inmates
- ✓ Write to a prisoner (never use your personal address, use a P.O. Box)
- ✓ Assist families of inmates, where feasible or practical
- ✓ Conduct worship services, Bible studies, or group meetings inside prisons under the supervision of the Staff Chaplain or prison administration
- ✓ Provide Scripture and literature for inmates
- ✓ Serve as a Volunteer Chaplain (without crossing lines into staff roles)
- ✓ Substitute for Staff Chaplains when they are ill or on vacation

CONDUCT A DEMOGRAPHIC ANALYSIS

Here are questions to answer in conducting your demographic analysis:

- ✓ What jails and prisons are in your immediate area?
- ✓ Is there a local ministerial association? What are they doing, if anything? Are they interested in jail or prison ministry? (If they already have a program and have gained access to local institutions, perhaps you can be a part of it).

✓ Who is in charge of the volunteers at the institution?
✓ How do you get clearance for ministry inside the institution? (Contact them and find out.)
✓ Are there forms you need to fill out?
✓ Does the institution have special training requirements?
✓ What identification must you have for clearance?
✓ What needs exist in their institution?

Familiarize yourself with all of the rehabilitation programs offered in the local institution where you wish to serve, as well as the population breakdown (race, religion, ages, sex, etc.) and, if possible, the philosophy of the respective administration. Gain as much knowledge as you can about the institution before requesting permission to provide services and/or programs. If you know administrators, officers, or former inmates, talk to them about the needs and conditions.

QUALIFICATIONS AND PREPARATION

Those who minister to inmates must be sure of their relationship with God, set proper examples, and always be ready to give an answer for the hope within them. While a person called to this ministry should demonstrate all of the spiritual virtues taught in the Word, this lesson emphasizes the spiritual qualifications a Volunteer Chaplain should possess.

SPIRITUAL QUALIFICATIONS

Courage

Entering a jail or prison to minister, whether on a one-on-one or group basis is outside of the "comfort zone" for most believers. It is not unusual to feel uneasy the first few times you are in a penal facility but remember, God will take care of you whenever you are in His service. In most cases, the Prison Chaplain is a safe place and the inmates are open and friendly. If you feel apprehensive, remember that God does not give a spirit of fear. Recognize where fear comes from and conquer it in the name of God! Hence, courage is a quality that is often associated with bravery, resilience, and strength in the face of adversity. In the context of chaplaincy, courage can be seen as the ability to confront difficult situations and to offer support and guidance to those who are struggling, even when it may be uncomfortable or challenging.

Chaplains often work in high-stress environments, where they are called upon to provide emotional and spiritual support to individuals who are experiencing significant challenges, such as illness, trauma, or incarceration. In these situations, it is important for chaplains to have the courage to face difficult emotions and to offer support and guidance with empathy and compassion.

At the same time, chaplains may also need to have the courage to confront difficult issues or to challenge unjust or unethical practices that may be present in their workplace or community. This may involve advocating for the rights of individuals who are marginalized or oppressed, or speaking out against policies or practices that are harmful or unethical.

Ultimately, the courage to act in the face of adversity is a critical aspect of effective chaplaincy. By demonstrating bravery, resilience, and a commitment to the well-being of others, chaplains can make a meaningful difference in the lives of those they serve.

COOPERATION

Cooperation is a fundamental aspect of chaplaincy that involves working together with others to achieve common goals and to provide support and care to those in need. In the context of chaplaincy, cooperation can take many forms, including collaboration with other chaplains or healthcare professionals, as well as working closely with individuals and communities to identify needs and develop solutions.

Effective cooperation in chaplaincy requires a willingness to listen to others, to be open to new ideas and perspectives, and to work collaboratively to find solutions to complex problems. This may involve working with diverse communities, including those from different cultural, religious, or social backgrounds, and being able to adapt one's approach to meet the unique needs of each individual or group.

In addition, cooperation in chaplaincy also involves a willingness to support others in their work and to be a team player. This may involve working closely with other chaplains, healthcare professionals, or volunteers to provide comprehensive care and support to those in need.

Ultimately, effective cooperation in chaplaincy is essential for creating a supportive and inclusive environment that promotes healing, well-being, and growth for all individuals and communities. By working together and supporting one another, chaplains can make a meaningful difference in the lives of those they serve.

Accordingly, there are many different persons in prisons society: Inmates, correction officers, nurses, doctors, social workers, teachers, captains, wardens and Chaplains, and we must not forget about the inmates' families. Most people we meet will probably treat us with courtesy and respect. Be sure to be courteous when speaking, shake hands when appropriate, and use names when reasonably possible. A good Volunteer Chaplain knows how to cooperate with other administration, volunteers, and Staff Chaplains if the jail or prison has one.

GENUINENESS

Be real! Inmates are adept at identifying phonies. We should not visit the prison with an improper motive like seeking a spouse or showing off our abilities. Wherefore, genuineness refers to being authentic and sincere in one's interactions with others. In the context of chaplaincy, it means being true to one's beliefs and values while respecting the beliefs and values of others. A genuine chaplain does not pretend to have all the answers or to be perfect, but rather acknowledges their own humanity and limitations while striving to be empathetic and supportive to those they serve. Genuine chaplains build trust and rapport with their clients by being sincere and authentic in their interactions and creating a safe space where individuals can feel comfortable expressing their thoughts and emotions.

Prisoners are extremely perceptive. They can quickly spot the person who joined the team out of curiosity. Those with selfish motives and "holier than thou" attitudes have no place in this ministry.

HUMILITY

Maintain a humble spirit. Remember, you are there to serve. Always be in subjection to those in authority (the Staff Chaplain, guards, and wardens). Humility is an essential characteristic for a chaplain, as it involves recognizing one's limitations and acknowledging the expertise of others. It means being willing to listen and learn from others, recognizing that no one person has all the answers. A humble chaplain does not seek to impose their beliefs or values on others but rather to support individuals in exploring their own beliefs and values. They are open to feedback and constructive criticism and are willing to admit when they are wrong. Humility allows chaplains to build trust and respect with their clients and colleagues and creates a safe and non-judgmental space for individuals to seek guidance and support.

FORGIVING

Foster a forgiving spirit. Recognize that, but for the grace of God, you could be in a similar situation. Realize that God's forgiveness extends to inmates. Therefore, forgiveness is a critical characteristic of a chaplain. In the context of chaplaincy, forgiveness involves helping individuals to let go of resentment and anger towards themselves or others. Chaplains can support individuals in exploring the deeper emotions that may be causing pain and suffering and help them find ways to forgive themselves or others. Forgiveness does not mean forgetting or condoning harmful actions but rather a process of letting go of the negative emotions that can prevent healing and growth. By promoting forgiveness, chaplains can help individuals move towards a sense of inner peace, reduce feelings of guilt or shame, and improve their overall well-being.

PERSEVERANCE

Society, friends, and family have given up on many inmates. They don't need someone else to reject them. Be patient. Volunteers who start and quit demoralize the inmates, disappoint the Chaplains and give a bad image to the efforts of the church. This is why perseverance is an essential trait for a chaplain. The work of a chaplain can be challenging, and often involves dealing with individuals who are going through difficult circumstances. Chaplains may face setbacks, obstacles, and resistance in their efforts to provide support and guidance to those in need. Perseverance is the ability to keep going in the face of adversity, to maintain a positive attitude, and to continue working towards one's goals. In chaplaincy, perseverance means continuing to offer support and hope to individuals, even when they may not be receptive or responsive. It involves staying committed to the chaplaincy work, even when it is difficult or frustrating, and continuing to show up for those in need, day after day. By embodying perseverance, chaplains can inspire others to persevere in their own struggles and can provide a source of hope and encouragement for those facing difficult times.

FAITHFULNESS

Be faithful, constant, and trustworthy on the performance of your duties, especially in keeping promises and being on time for appointments or service. The Prison Chaplain depends on you, as do the inmates. A visit that may just be another in a long list of things you have to do can be the highlight of an inmates' week. Don't disappoint them. Be faithful to this great privilege God has entrusted to you. Commitment to be consistent and dependable is a top-ranking quality valued by Staff Chaplains who work with Volunteer Chaplains.

Finally, faithfulness refers to the quality of being loyal, devoted, and committed to one's beliefs, values, and commitments. In the context of chaplaincy, faithfulness refers to the chaplain's commitment to their religious or spiritual beliefs and the ethical principles that guide their work. It also involves the chaplain's faithfulness to the individuals and communities they serve, including their willingness to be present with them through difficult times and to support them in achieving their spiritual goals. Faithfulness also requires the chaplain to be reliable, dependable, and consistent in their interactions with those they serve, building trust and rapport over time.

EMPATHY

Empathy is the ability to feel with people as though you were in their place. In the Old Testament, the Prophet Ezekiel sat with the captives by the River Chebar before he shared God's message to them. They were ready to listen, because they knew he understood. He had "sat where they sat." (Ezekiel 1:1). By definition, empathy is the ability to understand and share the feelings of another person. In the context of chaplaincy, empathy is a critical quality that enables chaplains to connect with those they serve on a deep emotional level. By putting themselves in the shoes of those they serve, chaplains can better understand their experiences, perspectives, and needs, and provide the appropriate emotional and spiritual support. Empathy also helps chaplains to create a safe and non-judgmental space for individuals to share their innermost thoughts and feelings, and to validate their experiences without trying to fix or change them. Empathy is essential in building trust, fostering meaningful relationships, and promoting healing and wholeness.

SENSE OF MISSION

A sense of mission is the feeling or belief that one's work or actions have a higher purpose or meaning beyond personal gain. In the context of chaplaincy and prison ministry, having a sense of mission means understanding and embracing the importance of the work being done and its potential impact on the lives of those being served.

Those who work in chaplaincy and prison ministry often have a deep sense of mission, feeling called to serve those who are often overlooked or marginalized by society. This sense of mission can provide motivation, direction, and purpose, even in the face of challenges and obstacles.

Having a sense of mission can also help chaplains and prison ministers stay focused on their goals and priorities, while avoiding distractions or temptations that could lead them astray. It can provide a sense of clarity and perspective, helping them to see the bigger picture and stay true to their values and beliefs.

Ultimately, a sense of mission can be a powerful force for good, inspiring chaplains and prison ministers to make a positive difference in the lives of those they serve, and helping them to stay committed and dedicated to their work over the long term.

SPIRITUAL GROWTH

You must not only lead inmates to new spiritual growth, but likewise you must be willing and anxious to grow. Spiritual growth refers to the process of developing and deepening one's spiritual life and beliefs. In the context of chaplaincy, spiritual growth is essential for chaplains to effectively minister to the spiritual needs of others. Chaplains themselves need to engage in spiritual practices, seek spiritual guidance, and continuously grow in their own faith and understanding.

Some ways chaplains can promote their spiritual growth include regular prayer, meditation, scripture study, attending religious services, and seeking mentorship or spiritual direction from a trusted advisor. Chaplains can also participate in continuing education and training to deepen their knowledge and skills in areas such as theology, pastoral counseling, and conflict resolution.

By focusing on their own spiritual growth, chaplains can bring a greater sense of authenticity, compassion, and empathy to their ministry, which can ultimately have a positive impact on the individuals and communities they serve.

EMOTIONAL MATURITY

With each day comes different feelings, trials, and tribulations but it is important that we handle our emotions and exhibit the fruit of the Spirit (Galatians 5:22-23), even when we do not feel that we are at our best. Emotional maturity is the ability to manage and understand one's emotions in a healthy way, even in challenging situations. It involves self-awareness, self-regulation, empathy, and social skills. In the context of chaplaincy, emotional maturity is crucial in building relationships with inmates, providing effective support, and navigating challenging or emotionally charged situations. Chaplains with emotional maturity can maintain a non-judgmental attitude, display empathy, and respond appropriately to the emotional needs of inmates. They can also handle their own emotions in a healthy way and prevent them from interfering with their work. Emotional maturity is a skill that can be developed through self-reflection, training, and experience.

LOVE

Study I Corinthians 13. The greatest motivating force behind any ministry, and especially prison ministry, is love. Your love for God, an unconditional love for the inmates and a love for the mission to which God has called you are very important. Love is a complex emotion that can take many forms, including empathy, compassion, and a deep sense of caring for others. In the context of chaplaincy, love is often expressed through acts of service, listening, and providing comfort and support to those in need. Love can also involve helping individuals to connect with their spiritual beliefs and finding meaning and purpose in their lives. Love is a powerful force that can help to heal and transform individuals, communities, and even the world.

PREPARATION

There are four vital areas of preparation for those who desire to be effective Volunteer Prison Chaplains.

Here are the four vital areas of preparation for those who desire to be effective volunteer prison chaplains:

1. Spiritual Preparation: To be effective as a volunteer prison chaplain, you must be spiritually prepared to offer spiritual guidance and support to inmates. This requires having a strong personal faith and relationship with God and being committed to ongoing spiritual growth and development. Regular prayer, Bible study, and participation in spiritual disciplines such as worship and fellowship are essential for spiritual preparation.

2. Emotional Preparation: Working in a prison environment can be emotionally challenging, so it's important to be emotionally prepared to handle the stress, trauma, and difficult emotions that may arise. This requires developing emotional resilience, empathy, and compassion, and being willing to seek out support and self-care when needed.

3. Educational Preparation: Effective volunteer prison chaplains should have a basic understanding of the criminal justice system, the issues facing incarcerated individuals, and the challenges of reentry. This requires ongoing education and training, including courses in theology, pastoral care, counseling, and criminal justice.

4. Practical Preparation: Finally, effective volunteer prison chaplains must be practically prepared to work in a prison environment. This includes understanding the rules and regulations of the facility, being familiar with safety and security protocols, and having good communication and

interpersonal skills. Volunteer chaplains should also have a clear understanding of their role and responsibilities, and be committed to working collaboratively with other staff members and volunteers to provide holistic care and support to inmates.

5. PRAYER PREPARE US

As in every ministry, effective prison ministry is fueled by prayer. Here are specific prayer targets:

- ✓ The Chaplains of the instruction.
- ✓ Individual inmates.
- ✓ Families of inmates.
- ✓ The warden and administrative staff.
- ✓ Correction Officers.
- ✓ Safety for prison volunteers entering the institution.
- ✓ For parolees' spiritual and practical needs (jobs, housing, etc.).
- ✓ Revelation knowledge to meet the needs of inmates.
- ✓ Many prison chapels have a prayer request box. Inmates write out their requests and put them in the box for the Staff Chaplain and Volunteer Chaplain to pray for their concerns.

STUDY OF THE WORD PREPARE US

The Volunteer Prison Chaplain should have good working knowledge of the Bible and basic Christianity. Most inmates are not interested in the finer points of theology, but they do need a clear, understandable presentation to help them learn to study and understand it? To be an effective Staff or Volunteer Chaplain, you must continually study God's Word. Therefore, studying the word of God can prepare us for various aspects of life, including spiritual and personal growth, ministry, and decision-making. The Bible contains principles and teachings that can guide us in our daily lives and help us develop a deeper relationship with God.

Through the study of the Bible, we can gain knowledge and understanding of God's character, His love for us, and His plan for our lives. This understanding can help us navigate life's challenges, make wise decisions, and live in a way that honors God.

Moreover, the study of the word can also help prepare us for ministry by equipping us with knowledge and insights into God's ways, His will for humanity, and the principles that underlie Christian living. It can also help us develop empathy and compassion for those we minister to, as we learn more about their struggles, fears, and hopes.

In summary, studying the word of God is essential for our spiritual growth, personal development, and effective ministry.

Readiness prepares us:

Being prepared and ready for any situation that may arise is crucial in any field of work, including chaplaincy. Readiness in chaplaincy involves being equipped with the necessary skills, knowledge, and tools to provide effective spiritual and emotional care to those in need. This includes being knowledgeable about different religions and cultures, having an understanding of human psychology and behavior, and being able to respond appropriately in crisis situations.

Readiness also involves being physically and emotionally prepared for the demands of the job. This means taking care of oneself through proper rest, exercise, and self-care practices. It also means being mentally prepared to deal with the challenges that may arise in the course of chaplaincy work, such as dealing with difficult individuals or situations.

By being prepared and ready for any situation, chaplains are better able to provide the support and care that individual in crisis or distress need. This can make a significant difference in the lives of those they serve, and help them to find the strength and resilience to overcome their challenges.

Knowledge of a specific Institution prepares us

There are five steps to prepare for the specific institutional setting you will enter:

- ✓ Know the rules for dress and conduct of the specific institution. These vary from institution to institution.
- ✓ Know the chain of command to which you are responsible as a Volunteer Chaplain.
- ✓ Know what you are allowed to take into the institution with you.
- ✓ Get a general understanding of the ways ministry can be carried out within that system.
- ✓ Attend training and orientation classes offered by the institution or Staff Chaplain.

RELATING TO INMATE

GUIDELINES FOR RELATING TO INMATES

Inmates have had a great deal of frustration in their lives. Many have experienced repeated failure and are suspicious of any offer of assistance or guidance. Working with inmates cannot be reduced to standard methods. Much will be left to your good judgment. Inmates often experience a great deal of frustration in their lives. Many individuals who end up incarcerated have faced significant challenges, including poverty, trauma, abuse, addiction, mental health issues, and a lack of access to resources and opportunities. These challenges can lead to feelings of hopelessness, anger, and frustration, which may contribute to criminal behavior.

Additionally, being in a prison environment can be extremely frustrating for inmates. They may feel powerless and restricted, with limited access to the outside world and few opportunities to make meaningful changes in their lives. The rules and regulations of the facility can also be frustrating, particularly if they feel unjust or overly restrictive.

As a volunteer prison chaplain, it's important to recognize and acknowledge the frustration that inmates may be experiencing. By offering a listening ear, showing empathy and compassion, and providing emotional support, you can help inmates process their feelings and begin to find hope and meaning in their lives. Additionally, by offering spiritual guidance and support, you can help inmates find a sense of purpose and connection to something greater than themselves, which can be a powerful antidote to frustration and despair.

Don't establish a facade or create special status for yourself.

Express yourself genuinely. Let the inmates know you are there out of genuine concern. As a Volunteer Chaplain you will be checked out and tested to see if you are real. Inmates will see who you are before they listen to what you say. They don't care how much you know until they know how much you care. Be honest. Inmates are very sensitive to hypocrisy and phoniest.

This is another important point to remember for those who want to be effective volunteer prison chaplains. It is essential to be genuine and authentic in your interactions with inmates. Creating a facade or pretending to be someone you are not can erode trust and credibility. It is also important not to create a special status for yourself, as this can create a sense of hierarchy and distance between you and the inmates. Instead, focus on building relationships based on mutual respect and shared humanity.

Learn as much of the prison related language as possible.

But be careful in using it. There may be subtle meanings of which you are unaware. Learning as much of the prison-related language as possible can be very helpful for volunteer prison chaplains. The prison environment has its own unique culture, customs, and language, and becoming familiar with these can help chaplains communicate more effectively with inmates and staff members.

Some examples of prison-related language include:

- "Cellie" or "cellmate": Refers to the inmate who shares a cell with another inmate.
- "The hole": Refers to the segregation unit, where inmates who have violated prison rules are often placed in isolation.
- "Chow hall": Refers to the cafeteria or dining hall where inmates eat their meals.
- "Canteen": Refers to the prison store where inmates can purchase items such as snacks, toiletries, and clothing.

- "Count time": Refers to the time of day when prison staff count the number of inmates in their cells to ensure that no one has escaped or is missing.

By learning these and other prison-related terms, volunteer prison chaplains can better understand the experiences and perspectives of inmates and staff members, and build stronger relationships based on mutual understanding and respect. It's important to remember, however, that each facility may have its own unique language and culture, so it's essential to seek out guidance and training from staff members and other experienced volunteers.

Learn to share your faith message in a clear and simple way. Big words such as "propitiation" and "atonement" don't mean much to the average inmate.

☐ Start with your personal story: Begin by sharing your own experience with faith and how it has impacted your life.

☐ Keep it simple: Use language that is easy to understand and avoid religious jargon that may be confusing to those who are not familiar with it.

☐ Listen actively: Ask questions to understand where the other person is coming from and tailor your message to meet their needs.

☐ Be respectful: Remember that everyone has their own beliefs and values, and it is important to approach conversations about faith with kindness and respect.

☐ Focus on the love: Emphasize the importance of love, forgiveness, and compassion in your faith message.

☐ Use examples: Share stories or examples from the Bible or your personal experience that illustrate your message.

☐ Offer hope: Share how your faith has given you hope and encourage others to find hope and meaning in their own lives.

Be sensitive during crisis periods.

During crisis periods, such as riots, fights, or deaths, it is important for a chaplain to be sensitive to the emotional needs of the inmates and staff. This includes being available to provide emotional support, offering prayers or spiritual guidance, and being a calming presence during chaotic situations. It is also important to work closely with correctional staff to ensure safety and security measures are in place during these times.

Mean what you say.

Yes, is yes and no is no. Be consistent and fair. Enforcing rules for some and relaxing them for others is inconsistent and unfair. It is also a form of overfamiliarity. Being genuine and sincere is an important aspect of effective communication and building trust in any relationship, including chaplaincy. When you say something, it is important to mean it and follow through on your commitments. This means avoiding making promises you cannot keep, being honest about your limitations, and being willing to admit mistakes or misunderstandings. When you are sincere in your words and actions, it helps to build rapport with the inmates and staff, and helps to establish your credibility and trustworthiness.

Be supportive, encouraging, friendly and firm.
Be honest, objective, and disapproving when it is warranted. Be friendly, but not overly familiar. Do not fraternize.

Being supportive, encouraging, friendly, and firm is crucial in prison ministry. The inmates are often dealing with various issues, including loneliness, fear, and hopelessness. They may feel disconnected from the outside world, and many have lost faith in themselves and others. Therefore, it is essential to be supportive and encourage them to build a better future for themselves.

At the same time, it is necessary to be firm with them, especially when it comes to maintaining the rules and boundaries within the prison. This helps to establish a sense of order and security, which is beneficial to both the inmates and the staff. Being friendly and approachable helps to create a comfortable atmosphere, which can make inmates more receptive to your message.

Respect is key.

You must respect the inmate's individuality and basic rights. Avoid prejudices and feelings of superiority. Respond to inmate's needs and interests, not your own. Once you have earned the respect and trust of the inmates, they will open up to you. Always remember that respect is indeed a crucial aspect of prison ministry. It is important to remember that inmates are individuals who have human dignity and should be treated with respect regardless of their past mistakes or current circumstances. This means listening to their stories, concerns, and needs with empathy, refraining from judgment, and being mindful of their personal boundaries. Additionally, it is important to respect the rules and regulations of the facility, as well as the staff and other volunteers who work there. A respectful and professional attitude can go a long way in building trust and rapport with both inmates and staff, and can ultimately contribute to a more positive and effective prison ministry experience.

Never allow residents to manipulate you with overdramatized stories of being falsely accused, unjustly incarcerated, or inhumanely treated.

These tactics are often used to arouse sympathy. (If you think the stories are true, and in some cases, they are, inform the inmate of your intention to share their story with the Chaplain on staff for handling.) As a volunteer prison chaplain, it's important to approach all interactions with inmates with compassion and empathy, but it's also essential to maintain a level of objectivity and not be manipulated by their stories. Some inmates may try to manipulate chaplains with overly dramatic or exaggerated stories of being falsely accused or mistreated, or may try to use their religion as a way to gain sympathy or special treatment.

While it's important to listen to the stories and concerns of inmates, it's also important to maintain professional boundaries and not allow yourself to be emotionally manipulated. It's important to remember that everyone has their own perspective and interpretation of events, and it's not the chaplain's role to judge or take sides in legal or disciplinary matters.

At the same time, chaplains can offer support and guidance to inmates who may be struggling with feelings of injustice or mistreatment and can help them find ways to cope with their circumstances in healthy and productive ways. By maintaining a compassionate yet objective approach, chaplains can be a source of strength and support for inmates while also upholding professional and ethical standards.

Inflammatory statements and careless remarks.

It is important to avoid making any inflammatory statements or careless remarks while engaging in prison ministry. Such statements can cause unnecessary tension or conflict with inmates, staff, or other volunteers, and can also undermine the credibility and effectiveness of your ministry. It is important to remain respectful, mindful, and tactful in your communication with everyone involved in the prison community.

Innocent or guilty.

Never assume an inmate is innocent or guilty and do not give legal counsel or advice.

As a volunteer prison chaplain, it is important to remember that whether an inmate is innocent or guilty of their crime, they are still human beings deserving of respect and dignity. It is not your role to judge or condemn them, but rather to offer spiritual and emotional support during their time of incarceration. Treating all inmates with impartiality and kindness can help create a safe and supportive environment for everyone involved.

Personal details.

Never reveal personal details, if you are privy to them, about the lives of staff or other inmates.

It's important to maintain appropriate boundaries and not disclose personal details beyond what is necessary for the ministry work. It's also important to respect the privacy of the inmates and not ask them to share personal details unless it is relevant to their spiritual or emotional well-being. In general, maintaining a professional and respectful demeanor is key in prison ministry.

Promises.

A good policy is to only make promises you know you can fulfill, and as few of them as possible. When refusing a request, explain why it is necessary to decline and express your regrets.

When volunteering in prison ministry, it's important to be careful with making promises to inmates. It's best to only promise what you know you can deliver, and avoid making unrealistic promises that may create false hope or disappointment. It's also important to be aware of the limitations of your role and the prison system, and to not make promises that go beyond what you are able to do. Instead, focus on being a supportive and caring presence, and offer help within the boundaries of what you are able to provide.

Avoid Familiarity.

One of the best ways to avoid familiarity in a group setting is to address each member of the ministry team, as well as the inmates, as "brother" or "sister" using first or last names.

Note: It's important to maintain appropriate boundaries and avoid becoming overly familiar with the inmates. This means avoiding physical contact that could be misinterpreted, avoiding sharing personal information that could blur the professional relationship, and avoiding behavior or language that could be seen as flirtatious or inappropriate. It's important to maintain a professional demeanor and treat all inmates with respect and dignity.

Do not give out your home address or telephone number.

Some institutions make it expensive for residents to make calls, even locally and you are often expected to pay the cost.

It is generally not advisable for volunteer prison chaplains to give out their home addresses or telephone numbers to inmates or their families. This is for safety and privacy reasons, as it can be difficult to know the intentions and motivations of individuals in a prison setting.

Instead, it's recommended that chaplains provide a designated contact point, such as an office phone number or email address, where they can be reached during specified hours. This helps to maintain professional boundaries and ensures that communication remains focused on the chaplain's role as a spiritual advisor and emotional support, rather than becoming overly personal or intrusive.

Additionally, it's important for chaplains to follow all facility guidelines and regulations regarding communication with inmates and their families. This may include obtaining permission from prison staff before contacting an inmate or their family members and adhering to specific protocols regarding the content and frequency of communication. By following these guidelines and maintaining appropriate boundaries, volunteer prison chaplains can provide valuable support and guidance to inmates while also ensuring their own safety and privacy.

Why The Resident is in Prison.

Never inquire as to why residents are in prison.

As a volunteer prison chaplain, it's important to respect the privacy and confidentiality of inmates and not inquire into the details of why they are in prison. In most cases, inmates will share their stories and experiences voluntarily if they feel comfortable and trust the chaplain.

However, it's important to remember that inmates are in prison to serve a sentence for a criminal offense, and that their past actions may have caused harm to others or violated the law. While it's not the chaplain's role to judge or punish inmates for their past actions, it is important to maintain professional boundaries and not condone or excuse criminal behavior.

Instead, chaplains can focus on providing emotional support, spiritual guidance, and opportunities for personal growth and transformation. By creating a safe and supportive environment for inmates to explore their beliefs, values, and motivations, chaplains can help them develop a sense of purpose and meaning that can facilitate positive change and help them successfully reintegrate into society upon their release.

Overfamiliarity.

Overfamiliarity can be a potential issue in prison ministry. It is important to maintain professional boundaries and avoid becoming too emotionally involved with inmates. This can lead to a lack of objectivity and compromise the effectiveness of your ministry. It is important to treat all inmates with respect and compassion, but to also maintain appropriate boundaries to avoid any misunderstandings or potential problems.

Transacting personal business for residents.

As a volunteer prison chaplain, it's important to maintain professional boundaries and avoid transacting personal business for residents. This includes tasks such as making phone calls, sending letters or packages, or handling financial transactions on behalf of inmates.

While it's understandable that inmates may need assistance with certain tasks, it's not the chaplain's role to act as a personal assistant or intermediary. Instead, chaplains can provide guidance and support to inmates in finding resources and support within the prison system, such as social workers or counselors who are better equipped to assist with specific needs.

By maintaining appropriate boundaries and referring inmates to appropriate resources, chaplains can avoid conflicts of interest and ensure that their role remains focused on providing spiritual and emotional support. This can help to build trust and rapport with inmates, while also upholding professional and ethical standards.

Your demeanor.

As a volunteer prison chaplain, your demeanor is important in creating a conducive atmosphere for ministry. You should maintain a calm and respectful attitude at all times, regardless of the situation. Avoid getting into arguments or confrontations with residents, as this can escalate into a security risk for everyone involved.

In addition, be aware of your body language and tone of voice, as they can communicate more than your words. Show that you are approachable and willing to listen, and maintain eye contact when speaking to residents.

Your demeanor should also reflect a non-judgmental attitude towards the residents. Remember that they are there to serve their sentence, and it is not your place to pass judgment on their actions. Instead, focus on ministering to their spiritual needs and providing emotional support.

Witnessing.

Never deliberately try to persuade prisoners to change their religious preferences. You are there to share your faith. Let the word make any changing that is necessary.

As a volunteer prison chaplain, witnessing or sharing one's faith is an essential part of the role. However, it is crucial to be respectful of the beliefs of the inmates and avoid imposing one's beliefs on them. It is important to listen to their perspectives, offer guidance, and provide an environment where they feel comfortable exploring their faith. Additionally, it is essential to be knowledgeable about different religious beliefs to avoid offending or disrespecting the inmates' beliefs. Ultimately, the goal should be to create an open and supportive atmosphere where inmates feel free to express their spiritual concerns and needs.

Respect.

Earn respect for yourself. Make it clear that you will not be manipulated. If a situation arises that you consider "borderline," check with prison officials to be sure of how it is to be handled.

Respect is one of the most important qualities to have when working with residents in a correctional facility. Here are some ways to show respect:

1. Listen actively and give the resident your full attention.
2. Use the resident's name when addressing them.
3. Use appropriate language and tone of voice.
4. Acknowledge the resident's feelings and opinions, even if you do not agree with them.
5. Treat the resident as an individual with unique needs and circumstances.
6. Show empathy and compassion.
7. Respect the resident's privacy and confidentiality.
8. Avoid making assumptions or judgments about the resident.
9. Be patient and understanding.
10. Be professional in your interactions with the resident.

Keep your composure.

An inmate overwhelmed with problems may confront you with hostility. At such times, do not force conversation upon him and don't respond in a hostile, sarcastic, or anxious manner. Keep your composure, ignore the hostility, or withdraw for a while. Chances are that the inmates will regain his composure. Always express unconditional love.

As a volunteer prison chaplain, it's important to remain calm and composed in all situations, even when faced with challenging or emotionally charged interactions with inmates. This can help to create a sense of stability and safety for residents, as well as maintain the chaplain's professional demeanor and authority.

One way to keep your composure is to practice mindfulness and self-care techniques, such as deep breathing or meditation, that can help to reduce stress and anxiety. It's also helpful to establish clear boundaries and guidelines for communication and behavior and to communicate these expectations clearly and consistently with inmates.

In situations where an inmate becomes agitated or confrontational, it's important to remain calm and avoid reacting emotionally. Instead, chaplains can use active listening and communication skills to understand the inmate's perspective and respond in a constructive and empathetic manner.

By maintaining a professional demeanor and responding calmly and compassionately in all situations, volunteer prison chaplains can create a safe and supportive environment for inmates to explore their spiritual and emotional needs. This can help to foster positive relationships and promote personal growth and transformation among residents.

Don't over identify.

Don't take the inmates' problems upon yourself. They are not your problems.

When working with inmates, it is important not to over-identify with them. This means that while you should be empathetic and understanding of their situation, you should not blur the lines between your own life and theirs. Over-identification can lead to unhealthy emotional attachments and can make it difficult for you to maintain professional boundaries. It's important to remember that while you are there to support and guide them, you are not their friend or family member. Maintaining a professional demeanor and treating everyone with respect is key to being effective in your role.

Don't expect thanks.

You may not receive thanks or any show of gratitude from an inmate. He may feel it, but may not know how to express it. Your effort, however, will be appreciated and rewarded by God.

As a prison ministry worker, it's important to remember that the work you do is not for recognition or thanks, but rather to serve the inmates and share the love of Christ. It's important to not have any expectations of being thanked or praised for the work you do, but to find joy in knowing that you are making a difference in the lives of others. Remember to stay humble and continue serving with a heart of love and compassion.

You must set limits.

Some inmates will push you until you say to stop. How hard and far they push will depend on what you allow. Don't compromise.

As a volunteer chaplain, it is important to establish healthy boundaries and set limits in your interactions with the inmates. This can include:

1. Time limits: Be clear about the amount of time you have to spend with each inmate, and try to stick to that time limit to ensure that you have enough time to minister to everyone who needs your attention.

2. Emotional limits: While it's important to be empathetic and supportive, it's also important to maintain emotional distance and not become too emotionally invested in the lives of the inmates.

3. Physical limits: Be mindful of your personal space and avoid any physical contact that could be interpreted as inappropriate or unwelcome.

4. Role limits: Remember that you are a chaplain, not a counselor or therapist. If an inmate needs more help than you can provide, refer them to the appropriate mental health professionals.

Setting these limits can help you maintain a professional and healthy relationship with the inmates while also ensuring that you are not overextending yourself.

Don't panic.

If you find yourself alone with an inmate, don't panic. As a prison minister, it is important not to panic in any situation. Panic can lead to irrational decisions and actions, which can result in harm to yourself or others. Instead, it is important to remain calm and think through the situation before taking any action. This may involve taking a moment to breathe, assessing the situation, and developing a plan of action that is safe and appropriate. In addition, maintaining a calm and composed demeanor can help to de-escalate tense situations and can set a positive example for those around you.

Leave your personal problems at home.

Inmates have enough problems of their own. They don't need to be burdened with yours.

As a volunteer prison chaplain, it's important to maintain appropriate boundaries between personal and professional life. This means leaving personal problems and concerns at home and focusing on the needs of inmates while on duty.

By maintaining a clear separation between personal and professional life, chaplains can ensure that their interactions with inmates are focused on providing spiritual and emotional support, rather than being influenced by personal issues or biases. This can help to build trust and rapport with inmates, as well as uphold professional and ethical standards.

If a chaplain is experiencing personal problems or stressors that may impact their ability to perform their duties effectively, it's important to seek support and resources, such as counseling or peer support, to address these issues. This can help to prevent burnout and ensure that the chaplain is able to provide the highest level of support to inmates.

Overall, leaving personal problems at home and maintaining appropriate boundaries is essential for volunteer prison chaplains to perform their duties effectively and create a safe and supportive environment for inmates to explore their spiritual and emotional needs.

Expectations.

In a temperate and tolerant manner, always imply that you expect the correct attitude from inmates.

As a volunteer prison chaplain, it's important to have clear expectations of yourself, as well as of the inmates and the prison staff you will be working with. These expectations can help to ensure that everyone is on the same page and working towards the same goals.

Some expectations that chaplains may have for themselves include maintaining professional boundaries, respecting the confidentiality of inmate communications, providing non-judgmental support and guidance, and upholding ethical and religious principles.

Expectations for inmates may include respecting the chaplain's authority and professionalism, participating in group and individual sessions, and following prison rules and regulations.

Expectations for prison staff may include maintaining open and respectful communication with chaplains, providing access to necessary resources and facilities, and collaborating to promote the well-being of inmates.

By setting clear expectations and communicating them effectively, volunteer prison chaplains can help to create a positive and productive environment for all parties involved. This can help to promote personal growth and transformation among inmates, as well as foster positive relationships between chaplains, inmates, and prison staff.

You must be a leader in the strongest sense of the word.

As a volunteer prison chaplain, it's important to possess strong leadership skills to effectively fulfill the duties of the role. This includes being able to inspire and motivate inmates, as well as collaborate effectively with prison staff and other volunteers.

Being a leader in the context of prison ministry means being able to provide guidance, support, and direction to inmates as they navigate their spiritual and emotional journeys. This may involve leading group sessions, providing one-on-one counseling and support, and coordinating with prison staff to ensure that inmates have access to necessary resources and support.

Strong leadership skills also involve the ability to build trust and rapport with inmates, as well as communicate effectively with them. This means being able to listen actively, provide non-judgmental support and guidance, and convey a sense of empathy and understanding.

In addition to these interpersonal skills, effective leadership in prison ministry also requires a commitment to ethical and professional standards, as well as a willingness to collaborate with others to achieve common goals.

Overall, being a leader in prison ministry means possessing a combination of interpersonal, organizational, and ethical skills, as well as a deep sense of compassion and commitment to serving those in need.

Your Conduct.

Never show that you have been angered by being profane, vulgar or abusive in any manner.

As a volunteer prison chaplain, your conduct is critical to building trust and establishing a positive relationship with inmates and prison staff. Your behavior and actions should reflect the highest standards of professionalism, respect, and ethical behavior.

This means maintaining appropriate boundaries with inmates and prison staff, and adhering to all prison rules and regulations. It also means maintaining confidentiality when working with inmates, and never sharing personal information or stories that could compromise their privacy or safety.

Your conduct should also reflect a commitment to promoting the well-being of inmates and creating a safe and supportive environment. This means being non-judgmental and respectful of inmates' beliefs and backgrounds, and providing support and guidance in a compassionate and non-coercive manner.

In addition to these basic standards of conduct, it's also important to be aware of any personal biases or prejudices that may impact your ability to effectively serve inmates. This requires ongoing self-reflection and a commitment to cultural competence and diversity.

Ultimately, your conduct as a volunteer prison chaplain should be guided by a deep sense of compassion, respect, and a commitment to serving those in need. By embodying these values and principles, you can help to create a positive and supportive environment that fosters personal growth and transformation among inmates.

Express appreciation.

Be appreciative when behavior has been commendable, for example, "You guys were great tonight, so attentive!"

Expressing appreciation is an important aspect of being a volunteer prison chaplain. It shows gratitude for the opportunity to serve and acknowledges the hard work and dedication of prison staff, fellow volunteers, and the inmates themselves.

Taking the time to express appreciation can have a powerful impact on the prison community. It can help to foster a sense of connection and support, and can motivate inmates and staff to continue their work with renewed energy and enthusiasm.

As a volunteer prison chaplain, there are many ways to express appreciation. This might involve writing thank-you notes to prison staff or fellow volunteers, recognizing the efforts of individual inmates who have made progress in their spiritual or personal development, or simply taking the time to offer a kind word or gesture of support.

Expressing appreciation should be an ongoing practice, rather than a one-time event. By regularly showing gratitude and acknowledging the efforts of those around you, you can help to build a positive and supportive community within the prison and contribute to the overall success of the prison ministry program.

Letters of Recommendation.

If a prisoner requests a letter of recommendation to judges and other criminal justice authorities, inform them that you will pass the request on to the Staff Chaplain for evaluation and possible action. As a volunteer prison chaplain, it's important to maintain appropriate boundaries with inmates and avoid engaging in activities that could compromise your neutrality or impartiality.

If a prisoner requests a letter of recommendation from judges or other criminal justice authorities, it's important to handle the request carefully and with sensitivity. In general, it's best to inform the inmate that you are unable to provide a letter of recommendation directly and that you will need to pass the request on to the Staff Chaplain for evaluation and possible action.

The Staff Chaplain is typically responsible for overseeing the spiritual and religious needs of the prison community, and may have established protocols in place for handling requests for letters of recommendation. By referring the request to the Staff Chaplain, you can ensure that it is evaluated objectively and without bias, and that all appropriate policies and procedures are followed.

In general, it's important to avoid engaging in any activities that could be construed as advocating for or against an individual inmate or group of inmates. This includes providing letters of recommendation or engaging in other activities that could be perceived as taking sides or showing favoritism.

By maintaining appropriate boundaries and referring requests for letters of recommendation to the appropriate authorities, you can help to ensure that your role as a volunteer prison chaplain is focused on providing spiritual guidance and support to those in need, rather than engaging in activities that could compromise your impartiality or neutrality.

Minister through personal counseling.

Counseling provides a friendly and supportive relationship for the one seeking answers or solutions to problems. This type of relationship can take place at the close of a worship service or Bible study session. Some prisoners may want to talk about what they heard or may have a problem to talk about. Most of the time, they are not actually seeking solutions. They just want someone to listen to and possibly bring encouragement and support.

As a volunteer prison chaplain, one of your most important roles is to provide personal counseling to inmates. Many prisoners are dealing with a variety of emotional and spiritual issues and may be struggling with feelings of guilt, shame, anger, or hopelessness.

Through personal counseling, you can help inmates explore their feelings and beliefs, identify areas of personal growth, and develop strategies for coping with the challenges of prison life. Some key principles to keep in mind when providing personal counseling include:

1. Listen attentively: Effective counseling requires active listening, empathy, and sensitivity. Be attentive to the inmate's verbal and nonverbal cues, and respond in a way that conveys your genuine interest and concern.
2. Build trust: Many prisoners have trust issues due to past experiences of betrayal or abuse. Work to establish a safe and confidential environment in which inmates feel comfortable sharing their deepest concerns and fears.
3. Respect boundaries: As a chaplain, you must be respectful of inmates' personal boundaries and avoid engaging in activities that could be perceived as inappropriate or unprofessional.
4. Offer guidance and support: Through personal counseling, you can offer guidance and support to help inmates make positive changes in their lives. Be prepared to offer spiritual guidance, practical advice, and referrals to other resources as needed.

By providing personal counseling to inmates, you can play a vital role in helping them to navigate the challenges of prison life, build stronger relationships, and develop a greater sense of hope and purpose.

Confidential Information.

You may have access to information which is confidential. You are not to reveal this information and it is not to be used for your own advantage or benefit. You must be able to deal with individuals' spiritual problems as if you know nothing about their crimes. Keep issues discussed in counseling confidential, unless they involve threats to someone's safety, including the inmates themselves. In this case don't tell them you are going to report it, but report it.

As a volunteer prison chaplain, you will often be entrusted with confidential information by inmates. It is essential that you maintain the highest levels of confidentiality and professionalism at all times.

Some key principles to keep in mind when dealing with confidential information include:

1. Respect privacy: Always be respectful of inmates' privacy and maintain the confidentiality of any information they share with you.
2. Follow institutional policies: Familiarize yourself with the prison's policies and procedures regarding confidentiality, and ensure that you comply with them at all times.
3. Use discretion: Avoid discussing sensitive information with other inmates or staff members, unless it is necessary to do so in order to ensure the safety and well-being of the inmate or others.
4. Seek guidance: If you are unsure about how to handle a specific situation or piece of confidential information, seek guidance from the staff chaplain or other prison authorities.

By maintaining strict confidentiality and professionalism, you can help to build trust and respect with inmates and staff members alike and ensure that you are able to continue providing effective spiritual guidance and support to those who need it most.

Be a good listener.

You don't have to answer to everything, but let the prisoners know that God does! If you think they need formal counseling, encourage them to seek it through institutional channels. And don't interrupt immediately if you think a statement is wrong. Listen!

One of the most important skills for a volunteer prison chaplain is the ability to be a good listener. Many inmates are dealing with deep emotional, psychological, and spiritual issues, and may not have anyone else to turn to for support and guidance.

To be an effective listener, it is important to:

1. Pay attention: Focus your attention on the person speaking, and make sure that you are fully present and engaged in the conversation.
2. Show empathy: Try to understand the other person's perspective and feelings, and show empathy and compassion for their situation.
3. Be non-judgmental: Avoid making assumptions or passing judgment, and instead focus on creating a safe and supportive space where the other person can share their thoughts and feelings.
4. Ask open-ended questions: Encourage the other person to share more about their experiences by asking open-ended questions that invite reflection and conversation.
5. Reflect and clarify: Reflect back to the other person what you have heard, and clarify any points that are unclear or confusing.

By being a good listener, you can help to build trust and rapport with inmates, and provide them with the support and guidance they need to navigate the challenges of prison life.

Don't make decisions for the inmate under any circumstances.

As a volunteer prison chaplain, it is important to remember that you are there to offer guidance and support, not to make decisions for the inmates you serve. While you can offer advice and share your insights, ultimately it is up to the inmate to make their own decisions.

Making decisions for an inmate can create dependency and can lead to negative outcomes. It is important to empower the inmate to make their own choices and to take responsibility for their actions.

Instead, focus on providing guidance, listening to their concerns, and helping them to explore their options. By doing so, you can help to build their confidence and self-esteem, and empower them to make positive changes in their lives.

Don't judge.

The ideas and appearance of the inmates are not to be judge, nor are their vocabulary, or manner of speaking. View inmates as individuals. Don't make assumptions based upon generalities or stereotypes. Categorizing an inmate is unfair and dehumanizing.

As a volunteer prison chaplain, it is important to remember that your role is to provide spiritual guidance and support, not to judge the inmates you serve. It is not your place to pass judgment on their actions or decisions that led them to be incarcerated.

Instead, approach each person with empathy and compassion, understanding that they may have experienced challenges and hardships that led them to make mistakes. By withholding judgment, you can create an environment of trust and acceptance that can be crucial to the healing process.

Remember that each person is unique and has their own story. Focus on their individual needs, rather than making assumptions based on their past or current circumstances. By doing so, you can help to create a safe and supportive space where inmates can explore their spirituality and find inner peace.

Don't scold or interrogate.

Many inmates already have poor self-image so don't scold or interrogate them about their previous condition or what they may have done to be placed in prison. Many already have poor self-image.

As a volunteer prison chaplain, it is important to approach your interactions with inmates with compassion and understanding. Avoid scolding or interrogating inmates, as this can be counterproductive and can create a negative atmosphere.

Instead, focus on listening to their concerns and providing guidance in a supportive and non-judgmental way. Encourage open and honest communication, but avoid pressuring them to share information they are not comfortable with.

Remember that many inmates may be struggling with difficult emotions or past traumas, and may be hesitant to open up. By creating a safe and supportive space for them to express themselves, you can help them to build trust and confidence in themselves and in the chaplaincy program.

Ultimately, your goal as a chaplain is to provide spiritual guidance and support to inmates, while respecting their individual needs and circumstances. By treating them with dignity and respect, you can help them to find inner peace and healing.

Be patient.

As a volunteer prison chaplain, it is important to approach your work with patience. Inmates may be facing a wide range of challenges, including emotional distress, mental health issues, and struggles with addiction. They may also be hesitant to open up to a stranger or may require time to build trust and rapport.

By remaining patient and understanding, you can help inmates to feel more comfortable and supported. This may involve taking the time to listen to their concerns, offering guidance and support, and being present for them in difficult moments.

Remember that the healing process is often slow and gradual and that it may take time for inmates to see the benefits of your work. By approaching your role with patience and persistence, you can help to create a more positive and supportive environment for inmates and support them on their journey toward healing and growth.

Don't be discouraged.

Above all remember, don't be discouraged. Do your best, pray and leave the results to God. Volunteer prison chaplaincy can be a challenging and emotionally demanding role, and it is important to remember that progress may be slow and difficult to measure. It is not uncommon to encounter setbacks or to feel discouraged at times, especially when working with individuals who are facing significant challenges.

However, it is important to maintain a positive attitude and to focus on the positive changes that you are able to effect, no matter how small they may seem. By maintaining a sense of perspective and staying committed to your work, you can help to create a more positive and supportive environment for inmates and contribute to their overall well-being.

Remember that you are not alone in this work, and that there are many resources available to help you stay motivated and engaged. Consider seeking support from other chaplains or mental health professionals, attending training and professional development programs, and reaching out to your community for support and encouragement. With patience, persistence, and a positive attitude, you can make a meaningful difference in the lives of the inmates you serve.

HOW TO AVOID BECOMING
THE VICTIM OF A SET-UP

To avoid becoming the victim of a set-up, here are some tips:

1. Be cautious of people who try to befriend you suddenly and without any apparent reason.
2. Be wary of people who try to get you involved in activities that you are uncomfortable with or that seem illegal or unethical.
3. Avoid sharing personal information with people you do not know or trust.
4. Trust your instincts and be wary of anyone who makes you feel uneasy or uncomfortable.
5. Be aware of your surroundings and the people around you, especially in unfamiliar or potentially dangerous situations.
6. Do not accept gifts or favors from people you do not know or trust.
7. If you suspect that you are being set up, talk to someone you trust and seek their advice.
8. Always be mindful of the potential consequences of your actions and be careful not to engage in behavior that could put you at risk of being set up.

WHAT IS A SET-UP?

A "Setup" is a situation where you are forced into compromising your own beliefs, standards, or institutional rules. You are forced or tricked into a compromising situation, and then taken advantage of by an inmate to receive favors or contraband like drugs, alcohol, etc.

HOW DOES A SETUP OCCUR?

A setup can occur in many ways, but typically it involves someone luring you into a situation where you may be falsely accused of a crime or wrongdoing. For example, someone might ask you to hold onto a package or run an errand for them without disclosing that the package contains illegal substances or that the errand is part of an illegal activity. Once you have been implicated, the person who set you up may attempt to use the situation to coerce you into doing something else or to gain leverage over you in some way. Setups can also occur in social situations or through online interactions, where someone may use deceitful tactics to manipulate you into a compromising situation.

A Setup usually proceeds as follows:

OBSERVATION

Inmates first observe your ability or inability to function under stress, your level of tolerance, whether or not you adhere to rules, and how effectively you will take command in a difficult situation.

Quicksand is a patch of sand that looks like any other on the surface, but it is a dangerous patch of ground that can suck you under and cost your life. It is not as it appears on the surface. This is often true in relationships. People are not always as they seem to be on the surface. While not all inmates are steeped in criminal behavior, many of them are and because of that, you must learn how to avoid setup in the instructional environment. Observation is the process of gathering information about a person, situation, or environment using one or more of the five senses. It is an essential tool for understanding and assessing situations, making decisions, and developing plans of action. Observation can be used to gather information about a variety of topics, such as individual behavior, group dynamics, environmental conditions, and more. It is a valuable skill for anyone working in a correctional or law enforcement setting, as it can help identify potential threats and risks, as well as opportunities for positive intervention and support.

TESTING

Before any conclusions can be drawn, inmates test their assumption about you in minor ways. This may include such things as unauthorized requests for supplies and materials, asking for favors, circumventing rules, preying on sympathy, or attempting to encourage you in intimate conversation. If you yield in these "minor areas," then you are a prime candidate for a setup.

THE SETUP

If you compromise minor rules or engage in ill-advised behavior, then an inmate can see an open door to set you up. They may threaten to tell the administration about your compromising guidelines in the past or try to trick you into doing something else that would violate the rules of the institution. They use this as a lever to get what they want such as contraband, like drugs or alcohol, or other inappropriate favors.

AVOIDING A SETUP

MAINTAINING A PROFESSIONAL ATTITUDE

Professionalism is a word used to describe a specific attitude towards ministry in jails and prisons. Professionalism means that your standards and lifestyle should be better than the standards and lifestyles of the majority of people confined to prison. You are not being professional if you use inmate jargon or break institutional rules as some inmates do. Maintaining a professional attitude is essential in avoiding a setup. Here are some tips:

1. Keep boundaries: Set and maintain professional boundaries with inmates, co-workers, and anyone else you interact with in the prison environment.
2. Stay neutral: Do not take sides in inmate disputes, and avoid engaging in gossip or other unprofessional behavior.
3. Follow protocols: Adhere to all institutional policies and procedures, including reporting any suspicious activities or behaviors to your superiors.
4. Be cautious: Do not share personal information or become too familiar with inmates or their families.
5. Keep records: Maintain accurate records of all interactions with inmates and others, including notes on conversations and incidents.
6. Be aware of your surroundings: Always be aware of your surroundings and trust your instincts if you feel uncomfortable or threatened.
7. Seek support: Seek support from your colleagues and supervisors, and do not hesitate to report any concerns or incidents to them.

By following these guidelines, you can maintain a professional attitude that will help prevent you from becoming the victim of a setup.

AVOID FAMILIARITY

One important way to avoid becoming a victim of a setup is to maintain a professional attitude and avoid familiarity with those you are working with. This means being friendly and approachable, but not becoming too personal or involved in the personal lives of inmates or other staff members. Maintaining professional boundaries can help prevent situations where someone might try to use personal information against you or manipulate you into doing something you shouldn't. It's important to be friendly and supportive, but also maintain a sense of distance and objectivity in your interactions with others.

REFUSE TO VIOLATE RULES UNDER ANY CIRCUMSTANCE

A setup always involves a previous infraction of rules. Refuse to violate rules under any circumstance.

Therefore, it's important to always uphold the rules and regulations in any situation, especially when working in a professional setting. Violating rules can not only put your job at risk, but can also compromise your integrity and credibility. It's important to prioritize the safety and well-being of yourself and others while also following the guidelines and protocols set in place.

REPORT ANY SETUP ATTEMPTS IMMEDIATE

If you are approached in this manner or find yourself ensnared in a setup, immediately report it to the Staff Chaplain or administration.

Reporting any setup attempts immediately is important in preventing the situation from escalating and protecting oneself from false accusations. It is essential to inform the relevant authorities, such as supervisors or the security department, and provide as much detail as possible about the incident. It is also essential to document any evidence or information that could support one's case and protect oneself from false accusations.

CONTACT WITH INMATES

GUIDELINES FOR CORRESPONDING

Here are some guidelines to help you correspond effectively with inmates. Keep in mind as you write to prisoners that many of them feel suspicious, resentful, and lonely.

Inmates are suspicious, because …

They have been abused or taken advantage of in past relationships. They may question your motive for writing: "What are you getting out of doing this?" Work at developing mutual trust, respect, and understanding. Inmates are often suspicious because of their environment and experiences. Being in a correctional facility can be a challenging and stressful experience. Inmates may have had negative experiences with authority figures in the past, including law enforcement, judges, and other officials. Additionally, they may have been betrayed or let down by friends or family members, leading to a general mistrust of others.

Furthermore, inmates may also be suspicious due to the nature of the correctional system. They are often in a situation where they have limited control over their lives, and their personal freedom is restricted. This loss of control can lead to feelings of powerlessness and vulnerability, which may manifest as suspicion and distrust of others.

In some cases, inmates may also engage in manipulative or deceitful behavior in order to gain an advantage or protect themselves from harm. This can contribute to an atmosphere of suspicion and mistrust among inmates.

Inmates are often resentful because …

Inmates can often become resentful due to their circumstances and the restrictions placed upon them. They may feel as though they have been unfairly judged or punished, or that the system is working against them. They may also feel a sense of loss, as they are separated from their families and loved ones, and are unable to participate in activities that they once enjoyed. Additionally, they may be dealing with issues such as addiction or mental illness, which can make their situation even more challenging. All of these factors can contribute to feelings of resentment and frustration.

If you so choose ...

You may write to an inmate but it is cautioned that you use a P.O. Box or your ministry's address to recruit and respond to correspondence.

Make it clear from the beginning that ...

You are not looking for romantic involvement. It is easy for inmates to become infatuated, even if they have never seen you. Kindness can be misinterpreted. If this happens, you should correct the issue immediately by reporting the matter to the Staff Chaplain or administration.

It is important to establish clear boundaries from the beginning of any interaction with an inmate. Making it clear that you are not looking for romantic involvement is a crucial part of maintaining a professional relationship. This can be done by setting clear expectations and boundaries, avoiding flirtatious behavior, and avoiding any situations that could be misconstrued as romantic or sexual in nature. It is important to remember that any type of romantic involvement with an inmate is strictly prohibited and could result in serious consequences for both parties involved.

It is suggested that you ...

Do not share anything about yourself, send any pictures, money or gifts to inmates.

Do not promise help with employment, housing, etc., after release from prison unless the ministry with which you are involved is adequately prepared to give it. Your purpose in writing is to be a source of encouragement in the Lord. Any request for social services should be channeled to proper prison release ministries; consult with the Staff Chaplain.

That is a good precaution to take as a volunteer or counselor working with inmates. It's important to maintain appropriate boundaries and avoid any behavior that could be perceived as favoritism or inappropriate relationship-building. This includes not sharing personal information, sending gifts or money, or engaging in any romantic or sexual activity with inmates. These actions can not only compromise your professional integrity but also put you at risk of violating rules or laws that govern interactions with inmates.

VISITING WITH INMATES

Many inmates have no one to visit them because family and friends:

- Live too far away or cannot afford to travel
- Have their own personal or financial problems
- Are ashamed of their loved one's incarceration
- Disapprove of their loved one's actions that led to incarceration
- Are estranged from their loved one
- Have passed away
- Are unable to visit due to their own health or disability issues.
  - live a great distance from where they are incarcerated;
  - do not have the necessary transportation / finances to visit;
  - have rejected them; or
  - do not exist.

Personal visits with inmates are one of the most rewarding areas of jail and prison ministry. This section explains its importance, details how to get involved, and offers guidelines for visiting individually with inmates.

VISITATION GUIDELINES

Here are ten visitation guidelines for visiting inmates:

1. Check the visitation rules and dress code before you visit.
2. Bring a valid ID, such as a driver's license, passport or state ID.
3. Arrive early for your visit and be prepared to wait in line.
4. Avoid bringing any prohibited items, such as drugs, weapons, or contraband.
5. Be respectful and courteous to the correctional officers and staff.
6. Do not bring children under the age of 18 unless they are on the inmate's approved visitor list.
7. Do not discuss the inmate's case or legal matters during the visit.
8. Avoid physical contact such as hugging or kissing, as it may be against the facility's rules.
9. Do not give or receive any items from the inmate during the visit.
10. Follow all instructions and guidelines given by the correctional officers and staff.
    - ✓ Go through proper channels to be approved by the institution as a visitor. You may have to fill out certain forms, be pre-approved before your first visit, carry a specific type of identification, etc.
    - ✓ Learn and abide by all visitation guidelines at the institution you are to visit. Rules may include days and hours of visitation, safety and dress codes, etc. They usually govern what can and cannot be taken into the institution with you. Many jails and prisons

have their rules in writing. Ask for them in advance of your visit, if possible.

  ✓ It is best to visit one-on one with a person of your same sex. This avoids the pitfalls of improper romantic relationships.

  ✓ Normally, it is best not to give money to an inmate or their family. If you believe there is a legitimate need and you really believe God is directing you to do this, it is best to channel your help anonymously through the Staff Chaplain or administration.

  ✓ Don't preach or lecture. Ask God to show you how to share His love in a way that will be accepted.

  ✓ If the institution permits, you may give religious literature directly to inmates. If not, give the material to the Staff Chaplain to deliver.

  ✓ Except if you have had professional training in the area of counseling, do not assume this role in the relationship. Additionally, don't feel you have to answer to every issue that is raised.

  ✓ Prison is a very impersonal, dehumanizing place and an inmate doesn't have much opportunity to receive individual attention. Make your visit positive and uplifting.

  ✓ Always remember you are there as a representative of God but don't spend all your time on spiritual matters. Foster a balanced visit.

GROUP MEETINGS

There are many types of religious meetings that can be conducted in a prison. However, they must be approved and supervised by the Staff Chaplain and/or administration. according to the First Amendment of the U.S. Constitution, prisoners have the right to practice their religion and have access to religious materials and services. Many prisons have religious programs and services available to inmates, including group meetings and worship services, but the specific rules and regulations can vary by facility. It is important for inmates to follow the guidelines and regulations set forth by their specific facility in order to participate in these programs.

- ✓ Worship Services
- ✓ Bible Study
- ✓ Music Classes (train vocalists, musicians or a choir for prison worship service)
- ✓ Musical or dramatic presentations
- ✓ Religious writings
- ✓ Discipleship classes for new believers

✓ Yes, that's correct. Religious meetings in prisons must follow specific guidelines and be approved by the prison administration. This is to ensure the safety and security of everyone involved and to prevent any unauthorized activities or behaviors. The Staff Chaplain and administration are responsible for overseeing and supervising all religious meetings, and inmates are required to follow all rules and regulations set forth by the prison. Some common types of religious meetings that may be allowed in prisons include Bible studies, prayer groups, and worship services.

CONDUCTING GROUP MEETINGS

Here are some guidelines for conducting group services in a jail or prison.

1. Obtain permission from the prison administration and the Staff Chaplain before conducting any group services.
2. Adhere to the prison's policies and procedures, including dress codes, arrival times, and approved items that can be brought into the facility.

3. Conduct yourself in a professional manner at all times and treat the inmates with respect.
4. Keep the focus on spiritual matters and avoid discussing personal or political issues.
5. Use appropriate language and avoid using slang or offensive terms.
6. Avoid making promises to the inmates that cannot be kept, such as promising to write letters or provide financial support.
7. Keep the service on schedule and avoid exceeding the allotted time.
8. Do not bring in any materials or items that have not been approved by the prison administration, including religious literature or music.
9. Do not provide any gifts or favors to the inmates.
10. Avoid discussing any personal information about yourself or your family.

TIMING

Correctional institutions run on a strict schedule. All group meetings should begin and end on time.

MUSIC

Music for worship in prison should be encouraging and uplifting. Songs that could be misunderstood as condemning or as "put down" should not be used, e.g., "Rescuing the Perishing." Neither should depressing music like "Nobody Knows the Trouble I've Seen." If you are using overheads, sing books or sound tracks, have these items ready. Always receive clearance from the Staff Chaplain before arranging musical activities which are different from that which your team normally does special groups, cantatas, etc.)

PRAYER

> Keep prayer short and to the point unless God moves in a special way. A lengthy prayer could not only

make the worship tedious but could be misunderstood by the prison as saying, "These people need long prayers."

- No particular position or posture is important, but when there is a large crowd (50 or more), it would be advisable to leave the congregation seated or standing while offering prayer rather than calling them forward to kneel. (This is for control purposes). relating to their families.

- Spend most of the time praying for the physical, social, mental and spiritual welfare of inmates, their concerns and those relating to their families. Pray also for institutional staff.

- It is okay to keep your eyes open a bit (or have a member of your team designated to keep their eyes open (for control purposes).

SCRIPTURE READING

The person reading Scripture is echoing the voice of God and setting the tone for the sermon or lesson. Have the text read with expression, reverence, and impressiveness (see Nehemiah 8:8). Announce clearly, before beginning to read, where the Scripture is located; book, chapter, and verse(s). Allow time for people to find the passage. Project your voice to those in the back of the room. Stand erect and speak clearly. Read God's Word so impressively that the prisoners' emotions will be stirred and their hearts turned heavenward.

Therefore, when reading scripture during a group service in a jail or prison, it's important to choose passages that are relevant to the audience and the theme of the service. It's also important to consider the language and translation of the Bible being used to ensure it is accessible to all participants.

Additionally, it's important to explain the context and meaning of the passage in a way that is clear and understandable for the audience. This can involve providing background information, explaining cultural or historical references, and relating the passage to current events or personal experiences.

Finally, it's important to allow time for reflection and discussion on the scripture passage, allowing participants to share their insights and perspectives. This can facilitate a deeper understanding and application of the scripture to their lives.

TESTIMONIES

If you are asked to give a testimony, do not view this as your golden opportunity to preach. Testimonies are a powerful way for individuals to share their personal experiences and how their faith has impacted their lives. When conducting group services in a jail or prison, testimonies can be a great way to encourage and uplift inmates. However, it is important to follow these guidelines:

1. Keep testimonies brief and to the point.
2. Encourage testimonies that are positive and uplifting.
3. Avoid negative or critical statements about individuals or institutions.
4. Ensure that testimonies are relevant to the theme or focus of the service.
5. Remind individuals to respect the confidentiality and privacy of others.
6. Provide opportunities for individuals to share testimonies in a safe and non-threatening environment.
7. If someone shares a particularly sensitive or personal testimony, encourage the group to respect their privacy and avoid discussing it outside of the group setting.
8. Finally, be sure to thank individuals for sharing their testimonies and remind them of the impact their words can have on others.

THE ABC'S OF TESTIFYING

Keep your testimony God-centered and follow the ABCs of testifying:

A - Always begin with your connection with God and how He has impacted your life. This helps establish your credibility and highlights the power of God in your testimony.

B - Be brief and to the point. Avoid going into unnecessary details that can distract from your main message.

C - Clearly communicate the message of the Gospel and the hope that can be found in Jesus Christ. Use simple language and avoid jargon that may not be understood by those who are not familiar with Christian terminology.

D - Depend on the leading of the Holy Spirit. Pray and seek God's guidance before sharing your testimony and trust in Him to guide you as you speak.

E - End with a call to action, encouraging others to seek a personal relationship with Jesus Christ and offering resources or next steps for those who may be interested.

F - Focus on the positive impact that your faith has had on your life and avoid negative comments about others or religious institutions.

PREACHING/TEACHING

Messages prepared for preaching/teaching in a prison should not exceed 30 minutes. Many inmates have limited attention span. You also want to leave enough time at the end of your message so that you can conclude it properly and have additional time with the residents. (Fellowship is important to them).

Make your message relevant to inmates. Adjust your presentation to what you know about your audience. Character building and encouraging messages are always good. When making a point about wrongdoing, always use "we" to include yourself.

When preaching or teaching in a jail or prison setting, here are some guidelines to keep in mind:

1. Stick to the approved topic and material.
2. Use language that is appropriate for the audience.
3. Avoid discussing controversial or divisive topics.
4. Be respectful of other religions and beliefs.
5. Use real-life examples to illustrate points.
6. Keep the message positive and encouraging.
7. Provide practical applications for the message.
8. Encourage questions and discussion.
9. Be aware of time constraints.
10. End with a clear call to action or invitation to further study.

THE FOLLOWING THINGS SHOULD NEVER BE DONE IN A MESSAGE:

- ✖ Never scold residents. Enough of this has been received from relatives, lawyers, judges, etc.
- ✖ Never make statements that can be misinterpreted by prison staff as a breach of security.
- ✖ Never downgrade other religions.
- ✖ Never present a "holier than thou" attitude.
- ✖ Never ask antagonistic questions or assume that the group disagrees with you.

THE FOLLOWING THINGS SHOULD BE DONE IN A MESSAGE:

- ✓ In small groups, whenever possible, use a circular seating arrangement.
- ✓ Also encourage class participation in small groups. The question-and-answer method is effective. Don't let one person dominate the conversation.
- ✓ Make sure everyone has the same literature and encourage them to read along.

✓   If you have to eject a disruptive student from a group, be tactful and courteous, but firm. If necessary, get the cooperation of the correctional officer(s).

RESPONSE

If you ask for a response from the group at the end of the message or that they rededicate their lives, be very clear about exactly what you want them to do and why. If you have a large group, it is best to have them raise their hands rather than come forward (security precautions).

INMATE PARTICIPATION

Inmate participation is an important part of group services in a jail or prison. Inmates should be encouraged to participate in discussions, ask questions, and share their thoughts and experiences related to the topic being discussed. However, it is important to maintain a respectful and orderly environment during the service, and the facilitator or leader should be prepared to redirect the discussion if it becomes too emotional or off-topic. Additionally, inmates should not be pressured to participate or share personal information if they do not feel comfortable doing so.

Encourage inmates to be a part of the service. For example, have an inmate sing a solo or share testimonies. Exercise caution with regard to the content and length of inmate participation. Keep in mind that you are working within a timeframe and you can only allow a minimum amount of resident participation at each service. If necessary, have a "waiting list." Be sure to screen songs that inmates want to sing, as some may not pick appropriate music. Always maintain control. Do not let any inmate take control of the group meeting.

Small group meetings, especially those dealing with the subject of addiction, provide an opportunity for all inmates to participate and share. If one inmate verbally attacks another in such sessions, intervene by directing the group back to issues rather than dealing with personalities.

FOLLOW-UP

Follow-up care for inmates who indicate their acceptance of God during an appeal at the close of a group meeting, or at any other time, is crucial. This may include:

1. Follow-up counseling sessions with a chaplain or religious volunteer
2. Access to religious literature and resources
3. Opportunities for further religious education or study
4. Referral to community religious organizations upon release

It is important to ensure that inmates have ongoing support as they continue to grow in their faith and make positive changes in their lives.

If possible, their names should be retained for your records as well as given to the Staff Chaplain. Encourage new believers to attend religious study sessions, religious services, and other uplifting opportunities offered in the institution.

New converts will be like young children taking their first steps. Most of the time, their environment will be alien and opposed to their new beliefs. Constant support, encouragement, and prayer are needed. They should:

- ✓ Be kept as spiritually active as possible by participating in worship services, religious studies, and other religious activities.
- ✓ Be given some responsibility in the ministry (as long as they are ready to accept it). Many are quite talented and their skills should be utilized for God's service.

A study of spiritual gifts will help them identify and begin to flow in the gifts God has given to them.

✓ Be encouraged to continue regular attendance at worship services and religious study sessions.

MINISTERING TO INMATE FAMILIES

It is not advised by this Chaplaincy that Volunteer Chaplains service inmates' families unless under the instruction and guidance of the Staff Chaplain or Administration. However, ministering to inmates' families is an important aspect of prison ministry. It can help alleviate the stress and anxiety that families experience while their loved one is incarcerated. Here are some ways to minister to inmates' families:

1. Provide emotional support: Families of inmates often feel a range of emotions, including shame, anger, and anxiety. Offering a listening ear and words of encouragement can go a long way in helping them cope with their feelings.

2. Offer practical assistance: Families of inmates may struggle with practical matters such as finances, transportation, and childcare. Providing assistance in these areas can help alleviate their stress and make their lives a bit easier.

3. Keep them informed: Families of inmates may feel disconnected from their loved one's life behind bars. Providing updates on their loved one's well-being, activities, and progress can help ease their concerns.

4. Pray with and for them: Prayer can be a powerful source of comfort and strength for families of inmates. Taking time to pray with and for them can help them feel supported and cared for.

5. Connect them with resources: There are many resources available to families of inmates, such as support groups and counseling services. Providing information on these resources can help them access the help they need.

HOW TO HELP INMATES' FAMILIES

Here are some ways you can help inmates' families:

1. Listen: One of the most important things you can do is to listen to their concerns and struggles. Sometimes all someone needs are someone to talk to.
2. Offer emotional support: Families of inmates often feel isolated and ashamed. Offer them emotional support by being there for them and showing them that you care.
3. Provide practical assistance: In addition to emotional support, families may also need practical assistance such as help with paying bills or transportation to visit their loved ones in prison.
4. Connect them with resources: There are many resources available to assist families of inmates, such as support groups and counseling services. Connect them with these resources to help them navigate the challenges they are facing.
5. Offer spiritual support: If the family is religious, offer to pray with them or provide them with spiritual guidance and support.
6. Advocate for their loved one: Families may not know how to navigate the complex prison system. Advocate for their loved one by helping them understand the legal process and advocating for their rights.
7. Be patient and non-judgmental: Remember that families of inmates are going through a difficult time. Be patient and non-judgmental in your interactions with them.

TRANSPORTATION AND HOSPITALITY

Provide transportation to and from the institution so the family can visit. If you live near a prison, provide a place for the family to stay overnight while visiting. Studies have shown that family members who keep in touch with inmates have influence in helping them readjust to society upon release.

Here are some ways to help inmates' families with transportation and hospitality:

1. Offer to provide transportation for the family members to and from the prison for visitation or other purposes.
2. Provide a place to stay for out-of-town family members who are visiting the inmate.
3. Offer to provide meals or groceries to the family members who may be struggling financially due to the incarceration of their loved one.
4. Assist in finding support groups or counseling services for the family members.
5. Be available to listen and offer emotional support to the family members who may be experiencing stress, anxiety, or other emotions related to their loved one's incarceration.

INFORMATION

The family may not know how to get information, such as trial dates; when and how to visit; or how to obtain legal representation. You can be a help in providing this information if you familiarize yourself with the system.

In general, finding information can be a challenge for families who are dealing with legal, medical, or other complex systems. Here are some tips on how to obtain information:

1. Ask for help: Don't be afraid to ask for help from professionals, such as lawyers, social workers, or healthcare providers. They may be able to provide you with information or refer you to someone who can.
2. Research: Do your own research online or at the library to find information about the legal or medical system you are dealing with. Look for reliable sources such as government websites or reputable organizations.
3. Attend meetings: Attend meetings or support groups related to the situation you are dealing with. This can be a good way to learn from others who have been in similar situations and get advice on how to navigate the system.

4. Contact relevant organizations: Reach out to organizations that specialize in the area you need information on, such as legal aid societies, patient advocacy groups, or community organizations.
5. Keep records: Keep detailed records of all communication, including dates, times, and names of people you spoke with. This can be helpful in keeping track of information and following up on any questions or concerns.

Remember, obtaining information can be a complex process, and it's okay to ask for help along the way.

SOCIAL SERVICES

Share information about public and private agencies whose function is to provide employment, legal aid, housing, financial assistance, counseling, education, etc. The family may also need assistance in applying for these programs.

Yes, social services can play a crucial role in providing support to families in need. As a chaplain, you can help connect families with relevant social service agencies and organizations that can provide them with the assistance and resources they need. Some common types of social services that may be helpful to families include:

1. Employment services: Many families may struggle to find work or may need assistance in finding job training programs. Social service agencies can help connect families with job opportunities and resources to improve their employability.
2. Legal aid: Families dealing with a loved one who is incarcerated may need legal representation or assistance with navigating the legal system. Social service agencies can help connect them with legal aid organizations or attorneys who can provide guidance and representation.

3. Housing assistance: Families may struggle with finding affordable housing or may need assistance with rent payments. Social service agencies can provide information about housing programs and resources to help families secure stable and safe housing.

4. Financial assistance: Families may struggle with meeting basic needs such as food, clothing, and utilities. Social service agencies can provide information about financial assistance programs and resources to help families meet their basic needs.

5. Counseling and mental health services: Families may need support and counseling to cope with the stress and emotional strain of having a loved one in prison. Social service agencies can provide referrals to counseling and mental health services.

By providing families with information about social services and connecting them with relevant agencies and organizations, you can help them navigate the challenges of having a loved one in prison and improve their overall well-being.

EMPLOYMENT

If the wage earner is incarcerated, the mate may need to find employment. That's correct. If the primary wage earner in a family is incarcerated, it can be a financial burden for their spouse or partner who may need to find employment to support the family. In addition, the cost of phone calls and visits to the incarcerated loved one can also add up, further straining the family's finances. There are some organizations that offer financial assistance and job training programs to families of the incarcerated to help alleviate some of these challenges.

HOUSING, FOOD, CLOTHING, AND FINANCES

The family may need temporary or permanent housing, food, and finances to help get them on their feet. If you or your House of worship provides financial help, checks should be used, if possible and made out for the bills involved, directly to the landlord, utility companies, etc.

That is correct. When providing financial assistance, it is best to use checks to ensure accountability and transparency. The checks should be made out directly to the bills or expenses involved, such as the landlord or utility company, rather than giving cash to the family. This helps ensure that the money is being used for its intended purpose and that there is a record of the transaction. It is also important to work with local resources and social service agencies to help the family find temporary or permanent housing, food, and other basic needs.

COUNSELING

The entire family or individual family members may need personal counseling in order to deal with the crisis. Yes, counseling can be very helpful for families dealing with the incarceration of a loved one. Counseling can help family members manage their emotions, cope with the challenges of having a loved one in prison, and develop strategies for moving forward. It is important to find a qualified counselor who has experience working with families affected by incarceration. Some resources for finding a counselor include contacting a local mental health clinic or community center, contacting a local chapter of a national mental health organization, or asking for referrals from trusted friends or family members.

PRESENTS ON SPECIAL OCCASIONS

Christmas and birthdays are difficult for children and their incarcerated parent(s). One way you can help is to purchase gifts for Christmas and birthdays, wrap them, and present them to the children from the incarcerated parent. This cheers up both inmate and child!

If you wish to give a gift to an inmate or an inmate's family member on a special occasion, such as a birthday or holiday, it is important to first check with the facility's policies and procedures regarding gifts. Some facilities have strict rules about the types of gifts that are allowed, such as only allowing items purchased from an approved vendor. Additionally, some facilities may have limits on the monetary value of gifts that are allowed.

If gifts are allowed, it is important to choose appropriate and respectful items. Avoid giving gifts that could be seen as inappropriate or potentially dangerous, such as sharp objects, weapons, or anything that could be used to facilitate an escape attempt. Consider giving gifts that promote positive behaviors and personal growth, such as books, educational materials, or art supplies.

It is also important to remember that gifts should not be used as a means of manipulating or gaining favor with an inmate or their family member. Gifts should be given out of kindness and a genuine desire to help, rather than as a way to exert control or influence over the recipient.

A HOUSE OF WORSHIP

The most important thing you can do for an inmate's family is provide a loving, supportive, accepting house of worship.

Yes, providing a welcoming and supportive house of worship can be incredibly valuable for the families of inmates. It can give them a sense of community, connection, and spiritual guidance during a difficult time. It's important to create an environment that is non-judgmental and accepting, as many families may feel ashamed or ostracized due to their loved one's incarceration. Providing resources for practical needs, such as job training, financial assistance, and counseling, can also be helpful in supporting families during this challenging time.

HOW TO CONTACT AN INMATE'S FAMILY

Contacting an inmate's family can be a sensitive matter, and it is important to respect their privacy and confidentiality. Here are some general guidelines:

1. Ask the inmate for permission to contact their family before doing so. Respect their wishes if they decline.
2. If the inmate agrees, ask for the family's contact information, such as their phone number or address.
3. Introduce yourself and explain why you are contacting them. Assure them that you are not sharing any confidential information about their loved one.
4. Listen to their concerns and offer support and resources if appropriate.
5. Respect their privacy and do not share their information with anyone without their permission.
6. Follow up as needed, but be mindful of their boundaries and wishes.
7. Remember that each family's situation is unique, and what may work for one family may not work for another. Be flexible and open-minded in your approach.

Check with the Staff Chaplain or administration at the jail or prison where you are ministering to see if there are rules against contacting an inmate's family or an established procedure you should follow. Also clarify the purpose of your contact.

Obtain written permission from the inmate so that the family and institution know you have the inmate's approval.

DRESS CODES IN PENAL SYSTEMS

Most penal institutions have specific dress and safety codes. Be sure to find out what they are before visiting the institution. In this section, you will learn the general dress codes applicable to all institutions. Some institutions prohibit visitors or volunteers from wearing colors that resemble inmates' or guard uniforms. Again, inquire about the specifics before visiting. It is advised by this Chaplaincy that Ordained Clergy and licensed Ministers wear Civic Attire.

Dress codes in the penal system refer to the rules and regulations governing the clothing and appearance of inmates, staff, and visitors within correctional facilities. The dress code policies vary depending on the facility, and they are designed to promote safety, security, and order within the facility.

For inmates, dress codes typically require them to wear a specific uniform or standard issue clothing provided by the facility. The uniforms are usually designed to be distinctive, durable, and easily identifiable, and they may vary depending on the level of security of the facility. Inmates may also be required to adhere to grooming standards, such as keeping their hair short and neat, shaving regularly, and maintaining good personal hygiene.

Staff members are also required to adhere to dress codes, which may include wearing uniforms or professional attire. Staff may also be required to adhere to grooming standards, such as keeping their hair neat and trimmed, and avoiding excessive jewelry or accessories that may pose a safety risk.

Visitors to correctional facilities are also subject to dress codes, which are designed to promote safety and security. Visitors may be required to wear modest, non-revealing clothing and avoid wearing gang-affiliated or provocative clothing. Visitors may also be required to undergo a search and screening process before entering the facility.

In summary, dress codes in the penal system are an essential component of maintaining safety, security, and order within correctional facilities. These policies help to promote a professional and respectful environment for inmates, staff, and visitors alike.

Appropriate Attire

Here are some general rules of appropriate attire applicable to all institutions:

1. Clothing should be clean, neat, and in good condition.
2. Avoid clothing that is too revealing, tight, or provocative.
3. Do not wear clothing that is too casual or athletic, such as shorts, tank tops, or athletic wear.
4. Avoid clothing with offensive language or graphics.
5. Do not wear clothing that is too dressy or formal, such as evening gowns or tuxedos.
6. Shoes must be worn at all times and should be comfortable and appropriate for walking.
7. Avoid wearing excessive jewelry or accessories that could be used as weapons or cause a security risk.
8. Hats and other head coverings may be prohibited, depending on the institution's policies.
9. Hair should be clean and well-groomed. Avoid hairstyles that could be used to hide contraband.
10. Follow any specific dress code policies issued by the institution.

✓ Do not wear tight, formfitting clothing.
✓ Do not wear low-cut necklines.
✓ Avoid T-shirts with emblems and slogans as an outer garment.
✓ No gang-related attire.
✓ Do not wear see-through or revealing clothing.
✓ No shorts.

For women:
✓ Dresses or skirts should fall below the knee.
✓ Avoid attire that reveals underwear straps. (Some institutions ban sleeveless dresses and blouses for this reason.)

✓ Choose dresses or skirts that are knee-length or longer. Avoid wearing anything too short or revealing. It's also important to avoid clothing that reveals your underwear straps or anything too low-cut or tight. Some institutions may ban sleeveless dresses and blouses, so it's best to check with the facility's dress code beforehand. Wear comfortable, closed-toe shoes and avoid high heels or sandals.

Generally speaking, wear attire that is appropriate in the business world. Ordained or licensed ministers should wear civic attire.

> "A good volunteer will follow institution rules, even if they seem to make no sense. One unruly volunteer can destroy an entire program by not obeying the rules."

POST PRISON MINISTRY

Some prisoners are released after serving their entire sentence as prescribed by law. In some legal jurisdictions, after completing part of their sentence, prisoners are eligible to go before a parole board. If granted parole before finishing their sentence, they are released with certain conditions, such as reporting regularly to a probation officer, not associating with ex-felons, and restrictions governing living and working arrangements. Conditions for release vary and are usually set by the court, a parole board, or parole officer.

Inmates being released from prison have many needs as they reenter society. This section will help you identify these needs, understand various types of post-prison ministries, and define your role in ministering to ex-offenders.

Post-prison ministry refers to the work of supporting and ministering to individuals who have been released from prison and are transitioning back into society. This can involve a range of activities, including providing resources and support to help them find employment and housing, offering counseling and spiritual guidance, and connecting them with community programs and services.

The goal of post-prison ministry is to help former inmates successfully reintegrate into society and avoid recidivism (re-offending and returning to prison). This can be a challenging process, as many formerly incarcerated individuals face significant obstacles such as limited job prospects, housing insecurity, and stigmatization. Post-prison ministry can play an important role in providing a supportive network and helping individuals navigate these challenges.

Some specific activities involved in post-prison ministry may include:

1. Job training and placement: Many post-prison ministries offer vocational training and job placement assistance to help formerly incarcerated individuals find stable employment and support themselves financially.
2. Mentoring and counseling: Mentoring programs and counseling services can provide emotional support and guidance to help individuals cope with the challenges of reentry.
3. Spiritual support: Many post-prison ministries offer spiritual support and guidance, which can help individuals find meaning and purpose in their lives and make positive changes.
4. Supportive housing: Some ministries provide transitional housing for individuals who are struggling to find stable housing after release from prison.
5. Community connections: Ministries may connect individuals with local community programs and services to help them access resources such as healthcare, legal assistance, and social services.

Post-prison ministry can be a powerful way to help individuals overcome the challenges of reentry and build a new life outside of prison. By offering support and guidance, these ministries can help former inmates become productive and contributing members of society.

THE NEEDS OF THE EX-OFFENDER

The needs of the ex-offender are multifaceted and can be different for each individual. However, some common needs of ex-offenders include:

1. Housing: Ex-offenders may have difficulty finding a place to live due to their criminal record. Providing assistance in finding suitable housing can be beneficial.
2. Employment: Ex-offenders may struggle to find employment due to their criminal record. Assistance in finding job opportunities, resume writing, and job skills training can be helpful.
3. Education: Many ex-offenders may not have completed their education due to incarceration. Assistance in obtaining a GED or further education can help them in obtaining employment.
4. Health and Mental Health Services: Many ex-offenders may have physical or mental health issues that need attention. Providing assistance in finding healthcare professionals and resources can help them lead a healthy life.
5. Substance Abuse Treatment: Many ex-offenders struggle with substance abuse issues. Providing resources and support for substance abuse treatment can help them overcome their addiction.
6. Financial Assistance: Ex-offenders may have difficulty making ends meet due to a lack of financial resources. Providing financial assistance or connecting them with financial resources can help them become self-sufficient.
7. Supportive Community: Ex-offenders may feel isolated and disconnected from their communities. Providing a supportive community can help them reintegrate into society and reduce the risk of reoffending.

Some inmates are blessed to be returning to supportive families and/or churches upon release from prison. If they do not have such support in place, then post-prison ministry is very important. Each person is different and has unique needs, but here are some common necessities most ex-offenders share upon discharge from an institution.

> Acceptance in a local church that is nurturing and supportive so they can develop spiritually. Invite them to go to church with you. Sit with them and invite them to have a meal or snack with you after service.

> Housing, food and clothing. Inmates who have no "street clothes" sometimes need a "parole box" containing clothes, underwear and shoes that they can wear when leaving the prison.

> Job training.

> Financial counseling, budgeting, etc.

> Family counseling is very important when ex-offenders are trying to reunite with their family.

> Additional personal counseling for addictions, such as drugs or alcohol abuse. Ex-offenders may find addictive temptations one of their first battles on the outside.

> If they have been incarcerated for a long time, they may need assistance with even simple decision making since inmates have very limited option for making decisions in prison.

> A strong support system and network of friends who will love and accept them, pray for and with them and help them work through problems.

In addition, find out as much as possible about the inmate before release. This knowledge will assist in post-prison ministry. Determine job skills and educational level. Find out where he is paroling to (sometimes it is required that an inmate go to a certain geographic location). Discuss plans with the Staff Chaplains and the appropriate institution authorities before you speak to the inmate about it. Do not promise anything if you cannot follow through on it.

POST PRISON MINISTRIES/RESOURCES

There are many post-prison ministries and resources available to ex-offenders to help them reintegrate into society and reduce the likelihood of recidivism. Here are a few examples:

1. Halfway houses: These are residential facilities where ex-offenders can live while they transition back into society. They often offer support services such as job training, counseling, and drug and alcohol treatment.

2. Job training and placement programs: Many organizations offer job training and placement programs specifically for ex-offenders. These programs help individuals develop new skills and find employment after their release.

3. Mentoring programs: Ex-offenders may benefit from having a mentor who can offer guidance and support as they reintegrate into society. Many organizations offer mentoring programs for this purpose.

4. Counseling and therapy: Many ex-offenders struggle with mental health issues related to their incarceration. Counseling and therapy can help individuals process their experiences and develop coping strategies.

5. Substance abuse treatment: Many ex-offenders struggle with substance abuse issues. Treatment programs can help individuals overcome addiction and prevent relapse.

6. Faith-based programs: Many churches and religious organizations offer programs specifically for ex-offenders. These programs may include support groups, mentoring, and job training.

7. Legal assistance: Ex-offenders may face legal barriers as they try to reintegrate into society. Legal assistance programs can

help individuals navigate these challenges and avoid legal trouble.

8. Community support: Simply having a supportive community can make a huge difference for ex-offenders. Many organizations offer support groups and other resources to help individuals connect with others who are going through similar experiences.

DETERMINING YOUR ROLE

What will your role be in post-prison ministry? It depends on the answers to the following questions:

1. What skills and abilities do you have to offer? Are you a good listener? Do you have counseling skills? Are you organized and able to coordinate events? Do you have teaching or mentoring skills?
2. What are the needs of ex-offenders in your community? Are there specific areas where you feel called to serve?
3. What resources do you have access to? Are there local organizations or government agencies that can provide support and assistance to ex-offenders?
4. What level of involvement are you willing and able to commit to? Do you have the time and energy to participate in ongoing ministry activities, or would you prefer a more limited role?

By answering these questions, you can begin to identify your role and the ways in which you can best serve ex-offenders in your community through post-prison ministry.

WHAT IS PERMITTED IN THE INSTITUTION IN WHICH YOU MINISTER?

Some institutions prohibit volunteers who minister inside the prison from working with inmates after their release. They reason that should the inmate return to prison, they might be too familiar with the volunteer or be shown special favors because of their relationship outside the institution.

Before beginning any post-prison ministry, it is important to check with the institution and find out what types of services and programs are allowed. Some institutions may only permit certain religious groups or may have specific guidelines for volunteer involvement. It is important to adhere to these guidelines in order to maintain a positive relationship with the institution and ensure that the ministry is effective.

WHERE ARE YOU MOST EFFECTIVE?

Are you more effective in ministering to inmates inside or upon release from prison? Where do your interests and vision lie? Which gives you the greatest joy and the greatest spiritual results?

It's important to assess where you can be most effective in post-prison ministry. Some individuals may be more effective in ministering to inmates while they are still in prison, while others may be better suited to working with ex-offenders who have been released. Consider your skills, interests, and experiences, and consult with other post-prison ministry leaders to determine where you can make the greatest impact. It's also important to remember that post-prison ministry is a team effort, and different individuals may have different roles to play in supporting ex-offenders as they reintegrate into society.

WHAT ARE YOUR TIME AND ENERGY LIMITATIONS?

You can't be everything to everyone. Due to personal time and energy restraints, you may need to confine yourself to ministering to inmates either inside or upon release, but not both. Additionally, it's important to be realistic about the amount of time and energy you can dedicate to post-prison ministry. It's important to set boundaries and prioritize your commitments in order to avoid burnout and maintain a sustainable level of involvement.

STARTING A POST-PRISON MINISTRY

Here are three steps for starting a post-prison ministry:
Step 1: Pray and Seek God's Guidance Before starting any ministry, it is essential to pray and seek God's guidance. Ask God to reveal His will and plan for your post-prison ministry. Seek counsel from other experienced ministers and church leaders. Research the needs of ex-offenders and how you can meet those needs.

Step 2: Develop a Ministry Plan Develop a ministry plan that outlines the goals, vision, and strategies of your post-prison ministry. Consider the resources you need, including volunteers, finances, and facilities. Determine the types of services you will offer, such as counseling, job training, and spiritual support. Identify potential partners and collaborators, such as other churches, non-profits, and government agencies.

Step 3: Build Relationships and Connect with Ex-Offenders To build a successful post-prison ministry, you need to build relationships with ex-offenders and their families. Attend re-entry events and seminars, visit halfway houses and re-entry programs, and connect with parole officers and other professionals in the criminal justice system. Attend court hearings and offer support to families of inmates. Establish a reputation for trustworthiness, confidentiality, and caring by consistently demonstrating a Christ-like attitude towards ex-offenders and their families.

STEP ONE: PRAY
- Prayer fuels all things.
- Pray about what God would have you do in the area of post-prison ministries.

STEP TWO: CONSULT YOUR SPIRITUAL LEADER

If you are a Pastor, consult with your board. If you are a church member, talk with your pastor. This is important for several reasons:

1. Your spiritual leader can provide guidance and support as you start your post-prison ministry. They may also have connections with other organizations or individuals who can assist you.
2. Your spiritual leader can help you discern if starting a post-prison ministry is within the scope of your church or organization's mission and resources.
3. Your spiritual leader can provide accountability and oversight to ensure that your ministry is conducted in an ethical and effective manner.
4. Your spiritual leader can also help you with training and resources for working with ex-offenders, and provide spiritual support for both you and the ex-offenders you minister to.

In summary, consulting with your spiritual leader is a crucial step in starting a post-prison ministry, as they can provide important guidance, support, and resources.

- ✓ It is common courtesy.
- ✓ Spiritual leaders can guide and provide valuable input.
- ✓ Your spiritual leader may already have plans underway for such ministry. If so, be a part of it, don't undermine it.

STEP THREE: DO AN ANALYSIS

Here are some questions to answer in your analysis:

- ➤ Are there any local post-prison ministries? If so, you may want to become a part of a post-prison ministry already in existence.
- ➤ What needs to exist in your community in regard to post-prison resources?

<u>NOTE</u>: If your institution does not permit your involvement with inmates upon release or you do not have the time or burden for post-prison ministries, then you will want to serve only as a referral agent. Make a list of churches, individuals, or Para-church organizations involved in post-prison ministries and refer inmates to them.

Whatever your involvement, your role should be that of a facilitator. Don't become a crutch for the inmate. Be available, but don't smother them. Encourage self-reliance. That's a great point. It's important to remember that post-prison ministry is about helping ex-offenders become self-sufficient and productive members of society, not enabling them to remain dependent on others. As a facilitator, your role is to provide support and guidance, but ultimately, it's up to the ex-offender to take responsibility for their own life and make positive changes. Encouraging self-reliance and personal growth should be a central focus of any post-prison ministry.

INSTITUTIONAL & INMATE TYPOLOGY

Institutional and inmate typology refers to the categorization of correctional facilities and the individuals who reside in them. There are several different typologies that have been developed, each with their own set of characteristics and classifications.

One of the most common institutional typologies is based on the security level of the facility. This includes maximum-security prisons, medium-security prisons, and minimum-security prisons. Maximum-security prisons are designed for the most dangerous and violent offenders, while minimum-security prisons are for non-violent offenders who are nearing the end of their sentence.

Inmate typology categorizes prisoners based on their criminal history, behavior, and other characteristics. This includes categories such as maximum-security prisoners, lifers, sex offenders, and those with mental health issues. Each of these categories requires specific programs and services to address the unique needs of the inmates.

Understanding institutional and inmate typology is important for developing effective programs and services that meet the needs of each population. It also helps to ensure the safety and security of correctional staff and the public.

Upon conclusion of this section, you will be able to:
- ✓ Demonstrate understanding of institutional security levels
- ✓ Discuss differences between jails, prisons, and other facilities
- ✓ Discuss common inmate typology

The following other key issues are addressed in this section:
- ✓ Are some inmates considered more dangerous that others?
- ✓ Are there any differences between a jail and prison?
- ✓ Do inmates share any common characteristics?
- ✓ How do you respond to someone who maintains their innocence?

Institutional Typology

Each jail and prison are unique, but most institutions are classified by the type of inmates they house: Here are some common institutional typologies:

1. Maximum-security prisons: These institutions house the most dangerous and violent criminals. The inmates in these facilities are typically serving long sentences for serious crimes such as murder, rape, or aggravated assault.
2. Medium-security prisons: These facilities house inmates who have committed less serious crimes or who have

demonstrated good behavior while in prison. They may have access to more privileges than those in maximum-security facilities, but they are still closely monitored.

3. Minimum-security prisons: These institutions house inmates who are considered low-risk and non-violent offenders. They may have more freedom of movement and access to certain programs, such as work-release programs.

4. Federal prisons: These institutions are run by the Federal Bureau of Prisons and house inmates who have violated federal laws. They include both maximum and minimum-security facilities.

5. County jails: These facilities house individuals who are awaiting trial or serving short sentences for minor crimes. They are typically run by local government agencies.

6. Juvenile detention centers: These institutions house minors who have committed crimes. They are designed to provide education, counseling, and other services to help rehabilitate juvenile offenders.

It's important to note that some facilities may be a combination of these types or may have their own unique classification system.

MAXIMUM-SECURITY INSTITUTIONS

These institutions house inmates that are at the greatest risk, perhaps due to the nature of their crime or their behavior in prison. Death row is usually located in maximum-security institutions. These inmates are very closely supervised and their participation in institutional programs run by volunteers is sometimes restricted.

MEDIUM SECURITY INSTITUTIONS

These institutions house less violent inmates who do not pose a great security or escape risk. They do not require as much supervision and may be allowed to freely participate in religious programs.

MINIMUM SECURITY INSTITUTIONS

These institutions house inmates who are close to their release date, incarcerated for non-violent crimes, or those who have proven themselves to be extremely reliable and trustworthy. They may even work outside the prison occasion and usually have the freedom to participate in religious programs.

Some institutions house all three security levels in separate areas of the same facility. Each of these levels is often found in jails also. Institutions sometimes clothe the inmates in uniforms of differing colors to identify the various security levels.

DIFFERENCES BETWEEN JAILS AND PRISONS

Although jails and prisons both house offenders, there are differences between the two. Prison inmates have been tried and convicted. Jail is usually the entry point for all prisoners. Many jail inmates haven't been convicted of anything yet. Most are being held awaiting trial. Some are being held pending sentencing. Some may be serving sentences so brief that it doesn't warrant sending them to prison.

Jails and prisons are both correctional facilities, but they differ in several ways. Here are some key differences:

1. Purpose: Jails are typically used to hold inmates who are awaiting trial, sentencing, or transfer to a long-term facility. Prisons are long-term correctional facilities where inmates serve their sentences.

2. Duration of Stay: Inmates in jails typically have shorter stays, ranging from a few days to a year or more, while inmates in prisons have longer stays, usually a year or more.
3. Size: Jails are usually smaller than prisons, with fewer inmates and staff. Prisons can house thousands of inmates and have larger staffs.
4. Security Level: Jails are usually lower security facilities, while prisons can have different levels of security depending on the type of inmate they house.
5. Funding: Jails are usually funded by local governments, while prisons are funded by state or federal governments.
6. Programs: Jails typically offer fewer rehabilitation and educational programs than prisons, which are designed to help inmates prepare for re-entry into society.
7. Inmate Population: Jails may house inmates with a wide range of charges, from minor misdemeanors to serious felonies, while prisons generally house more serious offenders.

OTHER TYPES OF FACILITIES

Some other types of programs of confinement include:

- Halfway Houses: Residential facilities for ex-offenders who have been released from prison and need help transitioning back into society.
- Juvenile Detention Centers: Facilities for youth who have been arrested and are awaiting trial or serving a sentence.
- Mental Health Institutions: Facilities for individuals with mental health issues who require treatment and care.
- Immigration Detention Centers: Facilities for individuals who are awaiting deportation or seeking asylum in a country.
- Military Prisons: Facilities for military personnel who have committed crimes while on active duty.

Work release centers allow inmates to hold a job in the community during the day and return to the center for confinement at night.

Half-way houses are for persons on parole. They are required to stay at the house while seeking employment and a permanent place to live. They may be required to complete certain counseling or training programs offered at the half-way house.

Road camps, fire camps, forestry camps, or work farms are programs where inmates work on roads, public forests, farms or fight fires.

Detention, juvenile hall, or reformatory are typically for young offenders to be kept separate from older prisoners.

Despite the distracting environment, jails, prisons, and other penal programs are some of the greatest spiritual harvest fields in the world. Jesus only had a few minutes with the dying thief on the cross, but his entire destiny was changed for all eternity.

INMATE TYPOLOGY

Each inmate is unique. God loves each one and is not willing that any should perish. There is no "typical" inmate in God's sight, but there are some common characteristics that will help you understand the majority.

Inmate typology refers to the classification of inmates based on their characteristics, behaviors, and needs. There are various typologies used to categorize inmates, and they are often used by correctional professionals to better understand and manage the inmate population. Here are some common inmate typologies:

1. Security Risk: Inmates who pose a high risk to the safety and security of the institution, staff, and other inmates.
2. Violence Risk: Inmates who have a history of violent behavior or pose a high risk of violent behavior.
3. Gang Affiliated: Inmates who are members of or affiliated with gangs.

4. Substance Abuser: Inmates who have a history of drug or alcohol abuse or dependence.
5. Mentally Ill: Inmates who have been diagnosed with a mental illness or disorder.
6. Sex Offender: Inmates who have been convicted of a sexual offense.
7. High-Profile Inmate: Inmates who are high-profile or well-known, such as celebrities or politicians.
8. Elderly Inmate: Inmates who are over the age of 55 and have special needs related to their age.
9. Inmate with Disabilities: Inmates who have physical or cognitive disabilities and require accommodations.
10. First-Time Offender: Inmates who are serving their first sentence and may have unique needs related to their lack of experience with the criminal justice system.

Education: often, the educational level of inmates is low.

Home environment: Inmates often come from homes where there was abuse, divorce, little supervision, and no discipline.

Vocational training: Many inmates have little or no vocational training. They may have been successful at obtaining or maintaining employment or labored at low paying jobs.

Self-Image: Inmates often have low self-image because society, friends and/or family has rejected them.

Emotional Profiles: Many inmates suffer from guilt over what they have done or put their families through. Depression, hopelessness, and hostility are common.

Social Responsibility: Inmates sometimes have limited sense of social responsibility. They may fell no remorse for their crime or that they got a "bad break" from the system by coming to prison.

Common Offenses: Four common crimes accounts for the majority of prison inmates in most countries: Robbery, burglary, murder, and narcotics violations. Other common reasons for incarceration are sexual offenses, kidnapping, assault, embezzlement, forgery, and fraud.

Inmate disruptions in ministry:

Beware that inmates also assume various disruptive roles in prison ministry:

Yes, unfortunately, some inmates may attempt to disrupt or manipulate the ministry for their own purposes. Here are some examples of disruptive inmate roles in prison ministry:

1. The Dominator: This type of inmate may try to dominate the discussion or take over the group, making it difficult for others to participate.
2. The Disrupter: This type of inmate may purposely disrupt the group by making noise, talking out of turn, or engaging in other disruptive behavior.
3. The Critic: This type of inmate may be overly critical of the ministry, the facilitator, or other participants, making it difficult to maintain a positive and supportive environment.
4. The Victim: This type of inmate may use the ministry as a platform to air grievances and seek sympathy, often overshadowing the needs of others in the group.
5. The Manipulator: This type of inmate may try to manipulate the ministry and its participants for their own personal gain, such as seeking favors or special treatment.

It is important to be aware of these potential disruptions and take steps to prevent or manage them in order to maintain a safe and productive ministry environment.

Hecklers may come to Bible class as earnest students but then disrupt the lesson by asking unanswerable questions. They may try to pour out scandalous stories about church and ministers or turn testimony time into a griping session. Maintain control of group sessions by continually bringing the group back to the subject at hand.

Perennial Seekers respond to every altar call due to a lack of understanding of what conversion is all about, a desire to please you, or because they have lived like a sinner since they last responded. Continue to receive them warmly when they respond and pray with them. When they are secure in their relationship with God and really understand conversion, a change will come.

Manipulators are those who may be charming and agreeable but try to use you for their own purposes.

Institutionalized Inmates are those who have been confined for a lengthy period of time and have difficulty functioning apart from an institutional setting. If they return to prison after paroling, don't be discouraged. They may be sincere in their confession to the Lord but just need more skills for adjusting to life outside.

Remember, these characteristics are not true of all inmates. Some are very educated and hold high-paying jobs. Some came from good homes and supportive families. Some are sincere seekers, desiring to learn about God. These general characteristics are based on numerous studies of the majority of prison inmates.

Most importantly, remember to view each inmate not as they were, or even as they are, but view them as the men and women of God that they will become when the Gospel has supernaturally impacted their lives!

ARE SOME INNOCENT

Many inmates maintain their innocence. For some who are guilty, this can be an escape mechanism. They cannot face what they did, so they rationalize or blame others. Some inmates who maintain their innocence actually are innocent! There have been many cases where inmates were released from prison after it was proven beyond a shadow of a doubt that they were wrongly convicted. This applies to former death row inmates also!

It is common for some inmates to maintain their innocence even after being convicted and serving time in prison. However, it is important to remember that the criminal justice system is designed to provide a fair and impartial trial process, and individuals are presumed innocent until proven guilty beyond a reasonable doubt. It is also important to recognize that there are cases where innocent individuals have been wrongly convicted, and efforts should be made to address these cases and prevent future wrongful convictions.

You are not to judge the guilt or innocence of an inmate. You are there to be a friend and minister God's love to them. Be supportive. Tell them you will pray that God undertake their case and that justice will be done.

Remember that, for various reasons, many heroes of the faith ended up with prison records. Joseph spent at least two years in prison after he was falsely accused of attempted rape (Genesis 39). Samson was imprisoned by the Philistines (Judges 16). Jeremiah was put into Ling Zedekiah's dungeon twice, once for unpopular preaching and once when falsely accused of treason (Jeremiah 32, 37).

In the New Testament, many of the apostles were thrown in prison by the Sadducees (Acts 5). Herod imprisoned John the Baptist (Matthew 4) and Peter (Acts 12), as well as Paul. The Apostle Paul had a lengthy prison record. He served sentences in Jerusalem (Acts 23), Caesarea (Acts 23), a local jail in Philippi (Acts 16), and in Rome.

Christians have been imprisoned throughout church history. John Bunyan and Dietrich Bonhoedder are two notable believers who were incarcerated. Modern China, Russia and Uganda have seen thousands of believers who were imprisoned and martyred.

Jesus said that being a faithful Christian may lead to prison (Matthew 10 and 24). Conversely, being a prisoner may also lead to faith, as one death row inmate discovered on Calvary.

HEALTHCARE CHAPLAINS

(Hospital / Hospice / Palliative Care / Nursing Home)
HOSPITAL CHAPLAINS

Healthcare chaplains are trained clergy members who provide spiritual care and support to patients and their families in hospitals, hospices, palliative care centers, and nursing homes. They offer a wide range of services, including counseling, prayer, sacraments, and emotional support.

The primary role of a healthcare chaplain is to provide spiritual care to patients and their families. They work closely with medical staff to ensure that the physical, emotional, and spiritual needs of patients are met. Chaplains may also provide support to staff members who are struggling with difficult situations or experiencing burnout.

Some of the specific services provided by healthcare chaplains include:

- Counseling and emotional support: Chaplains are trained to listen actively and offer emotional support to patients and their families. They may also provide guidance and counseling to help individuals cope with difficult situations.
- Prayer and spiritual guidance: Chaplains can offer prayer and other forms of spiritual guidance to patients and their families, regardless of their faith tradition.
- Sacramental ministry: Healthcare chaplains can administer sacraments such as communion, anointing of the sick, and baptism.

- End-of-life care: Chaplains can provide support to patients and families as they navigate end-of-life care decisions. They can also offer grief support to family members after a loved one has passed away.

Overall, healthcare chaplains play a vital role in providing holistic care to patients and their families. They work as part of a multidisciplinary team to ensure that all aspects of a patient's well-being are addressed, including their spiritual and emotional needs.

House Pastor for Staff

In the often stressful and demanding healthcare environment, the Chaplain is an understanding friend and confidant. The Chaplain can provide a listening ear and a pastoral point of view for the staff as they face professional and personal problems. Staff members who have no minister of their own often seek the Chaplain's counsel, especially during times of personal family need or professional pressures. As a Volunteer Chaplain, you may be asked at any time to minster to the hospital staff.

A healthcare chaplain may also serve as an in-house pastor for staff members. The chaplain can offer emotional and spiritual support to nurses, doctors, and other healthcare professionals who are dealing with difficult situations and stressors on a regular basis. The chaplain can provide a safe space for staff members to share their thoughts and feelings, offer guidance and encouragement, and help them find ways to cope with the challenges they face in their work. This can be particularly important in high-stress environments such as emergency rooms, intensive care units, and hospice care settings.

Liaison for Local Clergy

Usually, the Healthcare Chaplains on staff see patients/residents before their ministers are aware of the hospitalization. With the patient/ resident's permission, the Chaplain can call the family's pastor, priest, rabbi or other religious leader. The Chaplain provides pastoral care and support until the patient/residents own minister arrives. As a Volunteer Chaplain, you may be requested to take part in these services.

As a liaison for local clergy, Healthcare Chaplains can help connect patients or residents with their own faith community if they desire. They can also assist in coordinating visits from local clergy or religious leaders. Additionally, Healthcare Chaplains can work with local faith communities to provide additional support and resources to patients and residents, such as volunteer visitors, transportation to services, and spiritual counseling.

Contact for the Community

Serving often as the healthcare facility's religious public relations person, the Staff Chaplain is able to coordinate services provided by clergy for the community. The Chaplain is prepared to conduct seminars and workshops on topics such as patient/resident visitation, terminal illness, death, and the grieving process. The Chaplain is available also to speak in churches when the regular minister is away.

Furthermore, as a contact for the community, the healthcare chaplain can help coordinate religious services and support for patients and their families. This can include contacting local clergy to provide specific religious services or support for patients of a particular faith, as well as working with community organizations to provide additional resources for patients and their families. The healthcare chaplain can also help facilitate communication between the healthcare facility and the wider community regarding religious services and support available to patients and families.

Support for Patients/Residents' Families

The Staff Chaplain can provide emotional and spiritual support to the families of patients/residents who may be going through a difficult time. They can offer comfort, guidance, and prayer during times of distress and help the family members cope with the situation. The Staff Chaplain can also provide resources and referrals for additional support as needed.

Bereavement Counselor

It's important to note that while some Hospice Chaplains may provide bereavement counseling, it is not necessarily part of their primary role or duties. Bereavement counseling may also be provided by other members of the healthcare team, such as social workers or psychologists. However, Hospice Chaplains can provide spiritual and emotional support to both the patient and their family members during end-of-life care and may continue to provide support after the patient's death as needed.

Counselor

The counselor role is mentioned numerous times in relation to hospital ministry. It is seen by some Chaplains as the primary ministry and the ministry that is used initially when approaching a patient. A counselor is defined as a person who meets the patient's needs. The Chaplain's duty as a counselor is to discover the nature of the patient's needs at that moment and then meet those needs, whatever those needs may be. A counselor would therefore be primarily patient-directed and interested particularly in the patient's personal needs at the moment. Hence, it is not uncommon for healthcare chaplains to provide counseling services to patients, families, and staff members. They can offer emotional and spiritual support during difficult times, including illness, loss, and end-of-life care. Chaplains may also work with medical teams to address issues related to patients' psychological and emotional well-being. Counseling services can include individual or group sessions, as well as referrals to other healthcare professionals or community resources as needed.

However, the nature of the Chaplain as a counselor also bleeds over from counseling spiritual issues to counseling personal issues. Patients, for example, may need counseling on medical ethics or family problems while hospital employees may need counseling on their personal and work-related problems.

Comforter

The role of the Chaplain as a comforter is important in healthcare ministry. They offer emotional and spiritual support to patients and their families, especially in times of crisis, illness, or death. The Chaplain provides a listening ear, a calming presence, and offers prayers or religious rituals according to the patient's or family's wishes. Additionally, Chaplains can offer guidance and resources to those who may be struggling with spiritual or existential issues, helping them find meaning and hope in difficult situations.

Religious Functionary

As a religious functionary, the Staff Chaplain works to ensure that the religious and spiritual needs of patients and staff are met. They may perform religious services such as baptisms, weddings, or funerals, and may also provide support and counsel to those who are struggling with their faith or spiritual beliefs. The Staff Chaplain may also work with hospital administrators to ensure that the hospital's policies and practices are in line with religious and spiritual principles.

Ambassador of God

As an ambassador of God, the Chaplain is a servant, church representative, and witness. In times of crisis, the Chaplain assures God's love and concern. Often this role of ambassador is accomplished by mere presence. As God's representative, the Chaplain is able to show compassion, mercy, care, and love.

Some might specifically refer to this ministry as the ministry of presence, or as the "incarnational ministry." However, the Chaplain's ministry as an ambassador of God often goes beyond mere presence to also include the presentation of spirituality. Prayerfully leading a patient to a place where he or she expresses trust in God would be appropriate for the Chaplain in the role of ambassador.

Therefore, the Chaplain might have the role of an ambassador of God who, in the expression of that role, performs many functions. As an "ambassador," the Chaplain may function as a "counselor" in particular situations. The Chaplain in this role is still primarily an "ambassador" who is performing the "counselor" function.

Encourager

In this role, the Chaplain encourages patients to marshal their will to get better and helps them maintain their will to live. The Chaplain is there to help the patient see the things that are worth living for and the consequences of giving up too soon.

It's important to note that while encouragement is an important aspect of the chaplain's role, it should never come at the expense of the patient's autonomy or decision-making. The chaplain should work collaboratively with the patient, respecting their wishes and goals for their care, and not pressure them into certain choices or beliefs. Additionally, the chaplain should work within their professional boundaries and refer the patient to appropriate medical or mental health professionals when necessary.

Partner

In the role of partner, the Chaplain is to "join the sufferer, to enter the pain, to engage the absurdity, to descend into hell…not minimize or mitigate the suffering, but to help the sufferer to put the suffering in perspective." This ministry is identification with the patient and becoming a compassionate partner. The role of a partner is crucial in chaplaincy, as it involves empathizing with the patient and entering into their pain and suffering. The chaplain serves as a supportive presence and partner in the patient's journey, helping them find meaning and purpose in their experience. The chaplain is also there to help patients make sense of their suffering and to provide comfort and support as they navigate difficult emotions and experiences. This role requires deep listening and a willingness to be fully present with the patient, no matter how difficult the situation.

As is the case with this and all of the above roles, a Chaplain, in general, tries to be a compassionate partner with the patient and to go through the illness with them as a friend and a witness for God. However, too with all of these roles, the Chaplain cannot fulfill all of the requirements that the role demands. The Chaplain cannot fully enter into the sufferer's world but the Chaplain can point the sufferer to the one who is able to fully enter into his world.

> When serving as a Volunteer Chaplain in the Healthcare environment, one of the most important things to remember is: Never to meet with patients or groups alone (a staff member should always be present).

THE HOSPICE CONCEPT

The hospice concept is a type of end-of-life care that focuses on the comfort and quality of life for individuals who are terminally ill. Hospice care involves a team of healthcare professionals, including doctors, nurses, social workers, and chaplains, who work together to provide medical care, pain management, emotional and spiritual support, and practical assistance to patients and their families.

The hospice approach recognizes that the end of life is a natural and inevitable part of the human experience and aims to promote comfort and dignity for patients, while also providing support and guidance for their loved ones. Hospice care is usually provided in the patient's home, but can also be provided in hospitals, nursing homes, and hospice facilities.

The hospice team works closely with patients and families to develop a personalized care plan that addresses their unique needs and preferences. This may include pain management, symptom control, emotional support, and spiritual counseling. The team also provides practical assistance with daily activities, such as bathing, dressing, and meal preparation, as needed.

Hospice care is usually covered by Medicare, Medicaid, and many private insurance plans, making it an accessible option for many patients and families. Hospice services can be provided for as long as the patient's condition meets eligibility criteria and the patient and family continue to desire hospice care.

WHAT IS A HOSPICE CHAPLAIN?

A hospice chaplain is a trained spiritual care provider who offers emotional and spiritual support to patients and their families in end-of-life care. They work in hospice settings, providing spiritual counseling, emotional support, and guidance to patients and their families as they deal with the physical, emotional, and spiritual aspects of dying. Hospice chaplains are typically ordained ministers, but they can also be laypeople who have completed specialized training in spiritual care. They work closely with the hospice interdisciplinary team, including nurses, social workers, and doctors, to ensure that the patient's spiritual and emotional needs are being met. Hospice chaplains respect the patient's beliefs and preferences and work to provide care that is sensitive and supportive.

A Hospice Chaplain is a vital part of the overall Hospice team. The Hospice team usually consists of doctors, nurses, aides, social workers, Staff Chaplains and Volunteer Chaplains.

Although the Chaplain is not part of the medical team, the Chaplain is trained to have a listening ear and to be a comforting and supporting presence in a difficult time.

Hospice Chaplains on staff spend much of their time simply sitting with dying patients and listening to them talk. The Chaplains' most important duty is giving spiritual counseling and support. If requested, Chaplains may conduct religious services of their own faith, while refraining from proselytizing. Since hospice foundations receive government money, the services are required to be nondenominational. Hospice Chaplains visit the patient and family as often or as little as requested. Most visit the patient at least once a week. If the patient is active in church, the Chaplain stays in touch with the minister and other church members. They are also available for prayer or counseling. Volunteers who have received Hospice training may also assist the Staff Chaplains with servicing the family.

Role in the Hospice Team

The Hospice Chaplain plays an important role in the interdisciplinary team of healthcare professionals who care for patients who are at the end of their lives. They provide emotional and spiritual support to patients and their families, helping them to find meaning and peace in the final stages of life.

The Chaplain works closely with other members of the hospice team, such as nurses, social workers, and counselors, to provide comprehensive care to the patient and their loved ones. They help patients explore their beliefs and values, and provide spiritual counseling and guidance as needed.

The Hospice Chaplain also works with the patient's religious community or clergy, if applicable, to coordinate services and provide support. They may facilitate religious rituals or practices as requested by the patient or family, and can help connect them with appropriate resources and support systems.

Accordingly, the Hospice Chaplain serves as an integral member of the hospice team, providing comfort and support to those who are facing the end of life.

Misconceptions About Hospice Care

Here are some common misconceptions about hospice care:

1. Hospice care is only for the elderly: Hospice care is not just for the elderly. It is for people of any age who have a life-limiting illness and a prognosis of six months or less to live.

2. Hospice care means giving up hope: Hospice care does not mean giving up hope. It means shifting the focus from curative treatment to comfort care and making the most of the time remaining.
3. Hospice care is expensive: Hospice care is covered by Medicare, Medicaid, and most private insurance plans. Hospice care is also provided regardless of the patient's ability to pay.
4. Hospice care means being hooked up to machines: Hospice care focuses on quality of life and comfort, and not on the use of medical equipment or treatments that may cause discomfort or pain.
5. Hospice care is only for cancer patients: Hospice care is available to patients with any life-limiting illness, not just cancer.
6. Hospice care is only for the last few days of life: Hospice care can begin as soon as a patient is diagnosed with a life-limiting illness and has a prognosis of six months or less to live. Starting hospice care early can help patients and their families better manage symptoms and improve their quality of life.
7. Hospice care is the same as palliative care: Hospice care and palliative care both focus on improving quality of life and managing symptoms, but hospice care is specifically for patients with a life-limiting illness who have a prognosis of six months or less to live. Palliative care can be provided at any stage of an illness, even if the patient is still receiving curative treatment.

   ✘ It's expensive. Medicare and Private Insurance generally cover the full cost of Hospice Care. There are some exceptions, and your healthcare provider can help you figure out what will and won't be covered.

✗   It means you've failed in your fight against the disease. Hospice is not a judgment on your (or your doctor's) efforts. Hospice is an opportunity to choose how you want to spend your final days at home for example, rather than in a hospital.

✗   It means you will die soon. Wrong! Many people under Hospice Care live on for months. Hospice Care doesn't mean you should crawl into bed and die. Hospice Care is focused on making your final days comfortable and dignified.

✗   You have to wait until the very end. Although many hospice patients only take advantage of the care in the last week of life, Medicare covers six months of Hospice Care.

The choice to end life

Why might a person choose to not have Hospice Care at the end of life?

The answer is often financial gaps in Medicare and Private Insurance coverage. Things like intravenous nutrition and some chemotherapies are not covered. A person may have to stop using medications that can extend life (but not cure the disease) in order to enter Hospice Care.

There could be various reasons why a person may choose not to have hospice care at the end of life. Some of the reasons could include:

1. Personal preference: The person may have strong personal beliefs or cultural values that prohibit or discourage the use of hospice care.

2. Lack of knowledge: The person or their family may not have enough information about hospice care and may not fully understand the benefits of this type of care.

3. Fear: The person may have fears or misconceptions about hospice care, such as feeling that hospice care means giving up hope or that it may hasten death.
4. Financial concerns: The cost of hospice care may be a concern for some individuals, especially if they do not have insurance coverage or have limited financial resources.
5. Desire for aggressive treatment: Some individuals may prefer aggressive medical treatment, even at the end of life, and may not want to transition to hospice care.

It is important to note that hospice care is a personal decision, and individuals should be provided with adequate information and support to make an informed decision that best meets their needs and values.

GLOSSARY OF HOSPITAL /HOSPICE TERMS

1. The following are health and medical definitions of terms that are used in the Hospital/Hospice Environment: Hospice Care: A type of care provided to individuals with a terminal illness or condition in which the focus is on providing comfort and support rather than attempting to cure the illness.
2. Palliative Care: Care provided to individuals with a serious illness or condition with the goal of relieving symptoms and improving quality of life, but not with the goal of curing the illness.
3. Terminal Illness: A disease or condition that cannot be cured and is expected to lead to death.
4. DNR: An abbreviation for "do not resuscitate," indicating that the patient does not wish to receive cardiopulmonary resuscitation (CPR) in the event of cardiac or respiratory arrest.

5. Advance Directive: A legal document that outlines a person's wishes for medical treatment in the event that they are unable to communicate or make decisions for themselves.

6. Comfort Measures Only (CMO): A medical order indicating that the focus of care is on providing comfort to the patient, rather than attempting to cure the underlying condition.

7. Pain Management: The use of medication, physical therapy, and other techniques to manage pain in patients with chronic or acute pain.

8. Life-Sustaining Treatment: Medical treatments or interventions that are used to prolong life in patients with a serious or terminal illness.

9. Hospice Team: A group of healthcare professionals who work together to provide hospice care, including physicians, nurses, social workers, chaplains, and volunteers.

10. Respite Care: A type of care provided to caregivers of individuals with a serious illness or condition, allowing them to take a break from their caregiving responsibilities.

11. Bereavement: The period of mourning and grief following the death of a loved one.

12. Grief Counseling: Counseling provided to individuals who are experiencing grief and mourning following the death of a loved one.

13. Spiritual Care: Care provided to individuals with a focus on their spiritual and emotional needs, including counseling, prayer, and support from religious leaders.

14. Terminal Sedation: The use of medication to induce a state of deep sedation in a terminally ill patient who is experiencing uncontrollable symptoms, such as pain or agitation.

Abnormal: Outside the expected norm, or uncharacteristic of a particular patient. That definition of "abnormal" is correct. In a medical context, abnormal usually refers to something that deviates from the usual or expected range or pattern of a patient's health, behavior, or test results. It could indicate a condition or disease, or it could be a temporary or isolated deviation without significant clinical significance.

Acute: Of abrupt onset, in reference to a disease. Acute often also connotes an illness that is of short duration, rapidly progressive, and in need of urgent care. Yes, that's correct! The term "acute" is used to describe a medical condition or disease that comes on suddenly and is typically severe in nature. It is often used to contrast with chronic, which refers to a condition or disease that develops slowly and persists over a long period of time. Acute conditions may require urgent or emergency medical attention, while chronic conditions may be managed over a longer period of time with ongoing treatment and monitoring.

Acute Pain: Pain that comes on suddenly but has a limited duration. That's correct! Acute pain is typically caused by injury or inflammation and lasts for a limited period of time, usually less than six months.

Analgesic: drug that relieves pain. Yes, that's correct! An analgesic is a medication that is used to relieve pain. Examples of analgesics include over-the-counter pain relievers like acetaminophen and ibuprofen, as well as prescription medications like opioids.

Anemia: a red corpuscle deficiency in the blood. Anemia is a medical condition in which a person has a lower-than-normal number of red blood cells or hemoglobin in their blood, resulting in a reduced ability of the blood to carry oxygen. Symptoms of anemia can include fatigue, weakness, shortness of breath, and pale skin.

Anorexia: loss of appetite, resulting in the inability to eat. Anorexia is an eating disorder characterized by an abnormally low body weight, intense fear of gaining weight, and distorted perception of body weight and shape. It is not just a loss of appetite, but rather a complex psychological and medical condition.

Anticipatory grief: feeling of pain and loss before death has occurred. Anticipatory grief refers to the grief experienced in anticipation of a loss, typically the death of a loved one. It can involve feelings of sadness, fear, anger, and other emotions, and may occur when a person or their loved one has a terminal illness or is facing a life-threatening situation.

Antiemetic: a substance of procedure that alleviates nausea and vomiting. Yes, an antiemetic is a substance or medication that is used to prevent or relieve nausea and vomiting. It works by blocking signals to the brain that trigger these symptoms.

Appropriate death: the kind of death chosen for one's self. The term "appropriate death" usually refers to a death that is consistent with the individual's values, beliefs, and preferences. It may also involve the avoidance of certain medical interventions that the individual perceives as unnecessary or overly burdensome. Ultimately, what is considered an appropriate death may vary from person to person, depending on their cultural, spiritual, and personal beliefs.

Artificial nutrition and hydration: supplements or replace ordinary eating and drinking by giving a chemically balanced mix of nutrients and fluids through a tube placed directly into the stomach, the upper intestine, or the vein.

Auto-euthanasia: suicide. I'm sorry, but this definition is not accurate. "Auto-euthanasia" is not a commonly used term and does not mean "suicide." Euthanasia refers to the act of intentionally ending someone's life in order to relieve their suffering and is often used in the context of a terminally ill patient who is experiencing unbearable pain. The term "auto-euthanasia" could potentially refer to a situation where a patient intentionally ends their own life, but this is not a widely recognized or accepted term. It's important to note that suicide is a complex issue with many potential underlying causes, and should not be conflated with euthanasia.

Autopsy: examination of a body after death to discover the cause of death or extent of disease. Yes, an autopsy is a medical examination of a body after death to determine the cause of death or identify any diseases or injuries that may have contributed to it.

Autopsies are usually performed by a pathologist, who examines the body's organs, tissues, and bodily fluids to make a diagnosis.

Bereavement: period of grief after the death of a loved one. Correct! Bereavement refers to the state of grief and mourning after the loss of a loved one, as well as the period of time during which the bereaved person experiences these emotions.

Biopsy: microscopic examination of body tissue for diagnosis. A biopsy is a medical procedure that involves the removal of a sample of tissue or cells from the body for examination under a microscope. This is usually done to diagnose or rule out certain conditions or diseases, such as cancer or infection. The tissue or cells can be obtained through various methods, such as needle biopsy, surgical biopsy, or endoscopic biopsy.

Bolus: a dose of medication injected all at once. A bolus can also refer to a large amount of food or liquid that is swallowed quickly.

Bowel obstruction: something in the bowel preventing passage of stool. Bowel obstruction is a blockage in the small or large intestine that prevents or slows down the passage of stool or gas. It can be caused by a variety of factors such as tumors, scar tissue, hernias, inflammation, or twisting of the bowel. Symptoms may include abdominal pain, bloating, nausea, vomiting, and constipation.

Treatment options depend on the severity and cause of the obstruction and may range from medication and bowel rest to surgery.

Bowel regimen: instruction provided by a nurse to the patient and caregiver regarding ways to establish regular waste evacuation. Bowel regimen refers to a set of instructions given by healthcare professionals to patients or caregivers to establish regular bowel movements. This may include advice on diet, fluid intake, exercise, and medication to help prevent or relieve constipation or other bowel problems.

Breakthrough Pain: pain that occurs between dosages of narcotics analgesic for which a less potent medication is given until the narcotic can be given again. Breakthrough Pain is a type of pain that occurs despite regular use of pain medication. It is often a sudden and intense pain that "breaks through" the medication and can occur between doses. To manage breakthrough pain, a healthcare provider may prescribe a short-acting pain medication to be taken as needed in addition to the regular pain medication. This can provide more immediate relief of the pain.

CADD/PCA pump: CADD stands for "Continuous Ambulatory Delivery Device", which is a type of infusion pump used to deliver medication subcutaneously or intravenously.

PCA stands for "Patient-Controlled Analgesia", which is a method of pain management that allows the patient to self-administer small doses of pain medication through an infusion pump.

Competency, on the other hand, refers to a legal term used to describe a person's ability to make informed decisions, particularly related to medical treatment. It is determined by a court of law and is not interchangeable with CADD/PCA pump.

Cancer: An abnormal growth of cells that tend to proliferate in an uncontrolled way and, in some cases, to metastasize (spread). Yes, that is a correct definition of cancer. It is a complex disease characterized by uncontrolled growth and spread of abnormal cells in the body, which can lead to various symptoms and health complications. Cancer can affect any part of the body and has various types, with different causes, risk factors, and treatment options.

Capacity: In relation to end–of–life decision-making, a patient has medical decision-making capacity if he or she has the ability to understand the medical problems and the risks and benefits of the available treatment options. The patient ability to understand other unrelated concepts is not relevant. Correct. In medical ethics, capacity refers to a patient's ability to make informed decisions about their own medical care. A patient with decision-making capacity has the ability to understand their medical situation, the nature and purpose of any proposed treatment or procedure, the risks and benefits of each option, and the consequences of their decision. Capacity is determined by a healthcare professional, and the assessment should focus on the patient's ability to make a specific decision at a specific time, rather than on their general mental abilities.

Cardiopulmonary resuscitation: (CPR) is group of treatment used when someone's heart and /or breathing has stopped. CPR is used in an attempt to restart the heart and breathing. It may consist only of mouth to mouth breathing or it can include pressing on the chest to mimic the heart's function and cause blood to circulate. Electric shock and drugs also are used frequently to stimulate the heart. To add to the definition, CPR is a series of emergency procedures that are performed when a person's heart stops beating or when they stop breathing. The goal of CPR is to keep the blood flow and oxygenation to vital organs until advanced medical help arrives. CPR involves chest compressions, rescue breathing, and defibrillation (if needed). It is a life-saving technique that can be performed in a hospital or outside of a hospital setting.

Chemotherapy: oral or intravenous administration of drugs which kill cancer cells. Chemotherapy is a type of cancer treatment that involves the use of drugs to destroy cancer cells. These drugs can be given orally or intravenously and are designed to target and kill rapidly dividing cancer cells. Chemotherapy can be used alone or in combination with other treatments, such as surgery and radiation therapy, to treat different types of cancer. The specific drugs used and the duration of treatment depend on the type and stage of cancer being treated.

Chronic pain: a long lasting and continuous pain. Yes, chronic pain is defined as pain that lasts longer than three months or persists beyond the expected period of healing. It can be caused by a variety of factors, such as injury, illness, or nerve damage, and can have a significant impact on a person's quality of life.

Coma: an extended and deep state of unconsciousness. Yes, that is correct. Coma is a medical condition characterized by an extended and deep state of unconsciousness. Individuals in a coma are unresponsive to external stimuli, such as sound, touch, or pain. They may also have no sleep-wake cycle, and their eyes may remain closed or only open intermittently.

Coma can be caused by various factors, including traumatic brain injury, stroke, drug overdose, infection, or metabolic abnormalities. The severity and duration of the coma can vary depending on the cause and individual circumstances.

Treatment of coma typically involves addressing the underlying cause, monitoring vital signs, providing supportive care, and sometimes using medication to try to improve brain function. In some cases, individuals in a coma may gradually regain consciousness and recover, while others may have permanent brain damage and disabilities.

Committal Service: brief service at the grave side. Yes, that is correct. A committal service is a brief service that takes place at the graveside or the site where the remains of a deceased person will be laid to rest. This type of service is usually held after a funeral or memorial service and is meant to provide closure for family members and friends.

During a committal service, a final prayer or blessing may be said, and the casket or urn may be lowered into the ground or placed in a niche or mausoleum. Depending on the family's traditions and beliefs, there may also be readings, hymns, or other rituals performed.

The committal service is often a solemn and emotional occasion, and it provides an opportunity for loved ones to say their final goodbyes and pay their respects to the deceased.

Constipation: Infrequent and frequently incomplete bowel movements. Constipation is the opposite of diarrhea and is commonly caused by irritable bowel syndrome (IBS), diverticulosis, and medications. Paradoxically, constipation can also be caused by overuse of laxatives. Colon cancer can also narrow the colon and thereby cause constipation. A high-fiber diet can frequently relieve constipation. If the diet is not helpful, a medical evaluation is warranted. Yes, that is an accurate description of constipation. Constipation is a common condition that is characterized by infrequent and often incomplete bowel movements. The frequency and consistency of bowel movements can vary from person to person, but typically, if a person has fewer than three bowel movements per week, they may be considered constipated.

There are many potential causes of constipation, including a low-fiber diet, inadequate fluid intake, lack of physical activity, certain medications (such as opioids or anticholinergics), irritable bowel syndrome (IBS), and other medical conditions that affect the digestive system, such as diverticulosis, colon cancer, or thyroid disorders.

In some cases, paradoxically, overuse of laxatives can also lead to constipation. This is because the colon can become dependent on laxatives to function properly, and the muscles and nerves of the colon may become less responsive over time.

Treatment of constipation typically involves making lifestyle changes such as increasing fiber intake, drinking more fluids, and engaging in regular physical activity. Over-the-counter laxatives or stool softeners may also be used in some cases. If constipation persists despite these interventions, medical evaluation is warranted to rule out underlying medical conditions and to determine if prescription medications or other interventions may be necessary.

Curable: Amenable to a cure, capable of being cured, to being healed and made well. Most skin cancers, fortunately, are curable. The word cure is from the Latin cura meaning care, concern, or attention. Yes, that is correct. "Curable" refers to a condition that is amenable to a cure, which means it is capable of being healed or made well. Many medical conditions are curable, while others may be treatable but not curable, meaning that they can be managed or controlled but not fully eliminated.

In the context of healthcare, the term "cure" typically refers to the resolution of a disease or condition, often with the help of medical treatment or intervention. For example, many types of skin cancer can be cured with early detection and treatment, such as surgery, radiation therapy, or topical medications.

The word "cure" derives from the Latin word "cura," which means care, concern, or attention. This reflects the idea that curing a disease requires careful attention to the patient's condition, as well as the use of appropriate medical treatments and interventions.

Decubitus: inflammation or ulcer in the skin over a bony prominence (aka bedsore); plural; decubiti. Yes, that is correct. Decubitus, also known as a pressure ulcer or bedsore, refers to an area of inflammation, injury, or ulceration that develops on the skin over a bony prominence, such as the hips, heels, or buttocks. Decubitus ulcers typically occur in individuals who are bedridden or have limited mobility, as a result of pressure or friction on the affected area over an extended period of time.

The term "decubitus" is derived from the Latin word "decumbere," which means "to lie down." The plural form of decubitus is "decubiti."

Decubitus ulcers can range in severity from mild redness and irritation to deep, open wounds that can be difficult to heal. They can also increase the risk of infection and other complications, especially in individuals with weakened immune systems.

Prevention of decubitus ulcers involves regular turning and repositioning of immobile patients, as well as providing adequate cushioning and support to reduce pressure and friction on bony prominences. Treatment of decubitus ulcers typically involves wound care, including cleaning and dressing the affected area, and may also involve the use of medications to control pain or prevent infection. In severe cases, surgical intervention may be necessary.

Dehydration: excessive loss of water from the body tissue. Yes, that is correct. Dehydration is a condition that occurs when there is an excessive loss of water from the body's tissues. Water is essential for many bodily functions, including maintaining blood pressure, regulating body temperature, and facilitating the transport of nutrients and waste products throughout the body. When the body loses more water than it takes in, dehydration can occur.

Dehydration can result from a variety of factors, including sweating due to heat exposure or exercise, vomiting or diarrhea, excessive urination, or inadequate fluid intake. Symptoms of dehydration can range from mild to severe and can include dry mouth, thirst, fatigue, dizziness, and confusion. In severe cases, dehydration can lead to seizures, unconsciousness, or even death.

Treatment of dehydration typically involves replacing fluids and electrolytes that have been lost through sweating, vomiting, or diarrhea. This can be accomplished by drinking fluids that contain water and electrolytes, such as sports drinks or oral rehydration solutions. In severe cases of dehydration, hospitalization may be necessary to receive intravenous fluids and electrolytes.

Prevention of dehydration involves ensuring adequate fluid intake, especially during times of increased water loss due to sweating or illness. It is important to drink water and other fluids throughout the day, especially during hot weather or when engaging in physical activity.

Denial: refusal to believe that death will occur or has actually occurred. Denial can refer to the refusal to believe that death will occur or has occurred, but it is important to note that denial can also refer to a broader range of behaviors and emotions that individuals may exhibit when facing difficult or traumatic events.

In the context of death and dying, denial may manifest as a refusal to accept that a loved one is dying, a belief that the diagnosis is mistaken, or a reluctance to discuss end-of-life issues. Denial may be a normal and natural response to the shock and emotional upheaval of a terminal diagnosis or the death of a loved one.

However, persistent or prolonged denial can prevent individuals and their families from accessing appropriate medical and emotional support, and can also make it difficult to plan for end-of-life care or make important decisions. It is important for individuals and their families to acknowledge and address feelings of denial, and to seek the support and guidance of healthcare professionals or other resources, such as hospice care or grief counseling.

It is also important to note that denial can occur in a variety of contexts beyond death and dying, such as in response to traumatic events or other difficult life circumstances. In these situations, denial may serve as a coping mechanism to protect individuals from overwhelming emotions or feelings of helplessness. However, like denial in the context of death and dying, persistent or prolonged denial can prevent individuals from accessing the support and resources they need to move forward and heal.

Depression: An illness that involves the body, mood, and thoughts and that affects the way a person eats, sleeps, feels about him or herself, and thinks about things. Depression is not the same as a passing blue mood. It is not a sign of personal weakness or a condition that can be wished away. People with depression cannot merely 'pull themselves together' and get better. Without treatment, symptoms can last for weeks, months, or years. Appropriate treatment, however, can help most people with depression. The signs and symptoms of depression include loss of interest in activities that were once interesting or enjoyable, including sex; loss of appetite, with weight loss, or overeating, with weight gain; loss of emotional expression (flat affect); a persistently sad, anxious, or empty mood; feelings of hopelessness, pessimism, guilt, worthlessness, or helplessness; social withdrawal; unusual fatigue, low energy level, a feeling of being slowed down; sleep disturbance and insomnia, early-morning awakening or oversleeping; trouble concentrating, remembering, or making decisions; unusual restlessness or irritability; persistent physical problems such as headaches, digestive disorders, or chronic pain that do not respond to treatment, and thoughts of death or suicide or suicide attempts. The principal types of depression are called major depression, dysthymia, and bipolar disease (manic-depressive disease).

DME: durable medical equipment, i.e., hospital bed, bedside commode, wheelchair, special mattresses, oxygen, shower bench, and the like. Yes, that is correct. DME stands for "durable medical equipment," which refers to a category of medical equipment that is designed to provide therapeutic benefits to patients who have certain medical conditions or disabilities. Durable medical equipment is intended for long-term use and is typically used in a home setting, although it can also be used in other care settings, such as hospitals or nursing homes.

Examples of durable medical equipment include hospital beds, wheelchairs, walkers, oxygen equipment, commodes, shower chairs, and specialized mattresses. These devices can be prescribed by healthcare providers as part of a patient's treatment plan to manage symptoms, prevent complications, or improve function and mobility.

Durable medical equipment may be covered by insurance, including Medicare and Medicaid, although coverage may vary depending on the specific device and the patient's individual circumstances. It is important to work with healthcare providers and insurance companies to determine which devices are covered and how to obtain them.

Proper use and maintenance of durable medical equipment are important to ensure safety and effectiveness. Patients and caregivers should be trained in the proper use and cleaning of devices and should follow any instructions provided by the manufacturer or healthcare provider.

Do-not resuscitate (DNR) order: A do-not-resuscitate (DNR) order is a medical order written by a physician that instructs healthcare providers not to perform cardiopulmonary resuscitation (CPR) in the event of a cardiac or respiratory arrest. The order may also specify other medical interventions that should be withheld, such as artificial ventilation or defibrillation.

DNR orders are typically written at the request of the patient or the patient's family, and are intended for patients who are seriously ill or near the end of life. The decision to pursue or forego CPR is a deeply personal and complex one that should be made in consultation with healthcare providers and loved ones.

It is important to note that a DNR order does not mean that a patient will not receive any medical treatment in the event of an emergency or other medical crisis. Patients with a DNR order may still receive other medical interventions, such as pain management, antibiotics, or oxygen therapy, depending on their individual circumstances and treatment goals.

A non-hospital DNR order is a specific type of DNR order that is written for individuals who are at home or in another non-hospital setting, and who do not want to receive CPR. These orders may be signed by a physician, nurse practitioner, or physician assistant, and are typically kept in a visible location, such as on the refrigerator or near the patient's bed so that emergency responders can easily locate them in the event of an emergency.

Donor Card: specifies the way in which a person wishes his or her body utilized for medical purposes after death. A donor card is a document that indicates a person's wishes for organ and tissue donation after their death. It is a legal document that can be used to give permission for the donation of organs, tissues, and other medical components for the purpose of transplantation or research.

Donor cards can be obtained from a variety of sources, including hospitals, doctors' offices, and organ procurement organizations. They typically require the individual to provide their name, date of birth, and contact information, as well as information about their donation preferences.

The information on a donor card is legally binding and can be used to guide medical decision-making in the event of a person's death. It is important for individuals to discuss their donation wishes with their loved ones, and to carry a copy of their donor card with them at all times.

Donation of organs and tissues after death can help save or improve the lives of others, and is a powerful way to give back to the community. By completing a donor card and discussing donation wishes with loved ones, individuals can ensure that their wishes are respected and that they leave a lasting legacy of generosity and compassion.

Dyspnea: Dyspnea refers to a subjective sensation of shortness of breath or difficulty breathing. It is a common symptom that can be caused by a wide range of underlying medical conditions, including heart and lung diseases, asthma, chronic obstructive pulmonary disease (COPD), anxiety, and strenuous exercise.

Dyspnea can manifest as a feeling of tightness in the chest, rapid or shallow breathing, or a sensation of air hunger. It may be accompanied by other symptoms such as coughing, wheezing, or fatigue. In some cases, dyspnea may be a medical emergency requiring immediate attention, such as in the case of a severe asthma attack or a heart attack.

Treatment for dyspnea depends on the underlying cause and may include medications, oxygen therapy, breathing exercises, or lifestyle changes such as quitting smoking or losing weight. It is important for individuals experiencing dyspnea to seek medical evaluation and treatment to help identify and manage the underlying cause.

Emergency Medical Services (EMS): Emergency Medical Services (EMS) is a system of governmental and private agencies that provide emergency medical care to individuals in need, usually outside of healthcare facilities. The primary goal of EMS is to provide prompt, efficient, and effective emergency care to those who are injured or experiencing a medical emergency.

EMS personnel typically include paramedics, emergency medical technicians (EMTs), first responders, and ambulance crew. They are trained to assess and stabilize patients in emergency situations, provide advanced life support, and transport patients to appropriate medical facilities for further treatment.

EMS services may include emergency medical dispatch, which provides telephone guidance to callers in emergency situations, as well as mobile intensive care units and air medical transport for critically ill or injured patients. EMS personnel may also provide public education and training on topics such as CPR, first aid, and injury prevention.

EMS plays a critical role in the healthcare system, providing essential emergency care to individuals in need and helping to ensure that patients receive timely and appropriate medical treatment.

Emesis: Emesis refers to the act of vomiting or the material that is expelled from the stomach during vomiting. Vomiting is a reflex that helps the body to get rid of ingested substances that may be harmful or irritating. Emesis may occur due to a variety of reasons, such as viral or bacterial infections, motion sickness, pregnancy, certain medications, or medical conditions affecting the gastrointestinal system or other organs.

The material that is expelled during emesis may include partially digested food, stomach acid, and other stomach contents. In some cases, emesis may be accompanied by other symptoms such as nausea, dizziness, and sweating. Treatment for emesis depends on the underlying cause and may include medications to control nausea and vomiting, dietary changes, or other interventions to address the underlying condition.

Eulogy: A eulogy is a formal speech or written tribute that is delivered in honor of someone who has recently died. Eulogies are often delivered at funerals, memorial services, or other gatherings to honor and remember the life of the deceased person.

Eulogies typically include personal anecdotes and memories, as well as reflections on the life and accomplishments of the person being honored. The speaker may also offer words of comfort and support to family members and friends who are grieving.

Eulogies can be delivered by family members, friends, religious leaders, or other individuals who have a close relationship with the deceased. They may be delivered in a formal or informal style, depending on the preferences of the speaker and the nature of the gathering.

Therefore, eulogies are an important way to honor and remember the life of someone who has passed away, and to offer comfort and support to those who are grieving.

Euthanasia: Euthanasia is a highly controversial topic that involves intentionally ending a person's life in order to relieve their suffering from a serious illness or injury. There are two types of euthanasia: active euthanasia, which involves taking specific steps to end a person's life (such as administering a lethal injection), and passive euthanasia, which involves withholding or withdrawing treatment that would prolong a person's life.

In most countries, including the United States, euthanasia is illegal. However, there are some exceptions in certain states or countries where certain forms of assisted dying or physician-assisted suicide may be allowed under strict legal and ethical guidelines.

Proponents of euthanasia argue that it can help alleviate the suffering of terminally ill patients who are in great pain and have no hope of recovery. However, opponents of euthanasia argue that intentionally ending a person's life is unethical and goes against the principles of medical ethics and the value of human life.

It is important to note that there are alternative forms of end-of-life care available, such as palliative care and hospice care, which focus on providing comfort and support to patients who are nearing the end of their lives.

Grief: Grief is a natural response to loss and can involve a range of emotional, physical, and behavioral reactions. While the experience of grief can vary from person to person and depending on the nature of the loss, some common reactions include:

- Emotional: sadness, anger, guilt, anxiety, despair, numbness, shock, yearning, and sometimes relief
- Physical: fatigue, insomnia, changes in appetite, weight loss or gain, aches and pains, headaches, and other physical symptoms
- Behavioral: difficulty concentrating, withdrawal from social activities, irritability, restlessness, and changes in routines or habits.

Grief is a process that can take time, and there is no one "right" way to grieve. Some people may find it helpful to talk to friends, family, or a therapist about their feelings, while others may prefer to grieve more privately. It is important to take care of oneself during the grieving process, and to seek help if needed.

Healthcare Agent: A healthcare agent is a person appointed to make medical decisions on behalf of another person who is no longer able to make those decisions for themselves. This can occur when a person becomes incapacitated due to illness or injury and is no longer able to communicate or make decisions about their medical care.

A healthcare agent is typically designated in an advanced directive, which is a legal document that outlines a person's wishes for medical treatment in the event they are unable to make their own decisions. The healthcare agent is responsible for following the person's wishes as outlined in the advanced directive, and making decisions that are in the person's best interest.

It is important to choose a healthcare agent who understands and respects your wishes, and who is willing and able to carry out your wishes even in difficult or emotional circumstances. It is also important to discuss your wishes with your healthcare agent and other loved ones so that everyone understands your wishes and can work together to ensure they are honored.

Heroic measures: Heroic measures refer to emergency medical interventions that are used to sustain life in critical or life-threatening situations. These measures can include advanced cardiac life support (ACLS), cardiopulmonary resuscitation (CPR), mechanical ventilation, intravenous medications, and other interventions.

Heroic measures are typically used in emergency situations when a person's life is in immediate danger, such as in cases of cardiac arrest or severe trauma. They are intended to keep a person alive long enough to allow for more definitive medical treatment, such as surgery or specialized medical care.

While heroic measures can be life-saving, they are also invasive and can be uncomfortable or even painful for the person undergoing them. Additionally, they can be costly, and in some cases may not be effective in saving a person's life. As a result, it is important for individuals to discuss their preferences for medical care with their healthcare providers and loved ones in advance so that their wishes can be respected in the event of a medical emergency.

Hospice: Hospice care is a specialized type of healthcare that focuses on providing comfort and support to people who are nearing the end of their lives, as well as to their families and caregivers.

Hospice care can be provided in a variety of settings, including at home, in a hospice facility, in a nursing home, or in a hospital. Hospice care is designed to help manage a person's symptoms and improve their quality of life during the end stages of a terminal illness. This can involve pain management, symptom control, emotional and spiritual support, and practical assistance with daily activities.

In addition to providing care for the person who is dying, hospice also offers support and counseling to their family members and caregivers. Hospice care is typically provided by a team of healthcare professionals, including doctors, nurses, social workers, chaplains, and volunteers.

Hospice care is generally covered by Medicare and many private insurance plans, and is available to people of all ages who are diagnosed with a terminal illness and have a life expectancy of six months or less. However, it is important to note that hospice care is not intended to hasten or prolong death, but rather to improve the quality of life for people who are nearing the end of their lives.

Hospice Care: Hospice care is all about improving the quality of life for patients with a terminal illness, by managing their symptoms, providing emotional and spiritual support, and ensuring that their wishes and preferences are respected. Hospice care is generally provided by a team of professionals, including doctors, nurses, social workers, chaplains, and volunteers, who work together to meet the unique needs of each patient and their family.

ICU: The ICU, or intensive care unit, is a specialized unit in a hospital that provides comprehensive and continuous care for critically ill patients who require close monitoring and support of their vital functions. The ICU is staffed by a team of healthcare professionals, including doctors, nurses, respiratory therapists, and other specialists who are trained in managing life-threatening conditions and complications. Patients in the ICU may require mechanical ventilation, hemodynamic monitoring, dialysis, or other advanced interventions to support their vital organs and maintain their stability.

Incurable: "Incurable" refers to a medical condition that cannot be cured or healed completely, such as certain types of cancer or chronic diseases. While medical treatments and interventions may help manage symptoms or slow the progression of the disease, the underlying condition remains present and cannot be completely eliminated.

Injury: While injuries may include wounds and trauma, they are not necessarily synonymous. An injury is a broader term that encompasses any harm or damage, whether it is physical or psychological, caused by an external agent or an internal factor, such as a disease or a medical condition.

Inpatient: A patient whose care requires a stay in a hospital; as opposed to an outpatient. The term inpatient dates back to at least 1760. The term "inpatient" has been used for several centuries to refer to a person who receives medical treatment while staying in a hospital. The term "outpatient," on the other hand, is used to describe a person who receives medical treatment without being admitted to the hospital and who is able to go home the same day.

Intubation: Endotracheal intubation is a medical procedure that involves the insertion of a flexible plastic tube through the mouth or nose into the trachea to create an airway. The tube is then connected to a ventilator or breathing machine to assist with breathing. Intubation is commonly used in emergency and critical care settings, as well as during surgery, to ensure adequate oxygenation and ventilation.

Inquest: An inquest is a formal legal inquiry into the circumstances surrounding a death. It is conducted by a coroner or other legal authority and aims to determine the cause of death and any contributing factors. The inquest may involve testimony from witnesses and experts, examination of evidence, and review of medical records. The findings of an inquest may be used in legal proceedings, and may also provide closure and answers for the family and loved ones of the deceased.

Life-sustaining treatment: medical procedures that replace or support an essential bodily function (may also be called life support treatment). Life-sustaining treatments include cardiopulmonary resuscitation, mechanical ventilation, artificial nutrition and hydration, dialysis, and other treatments. Furthermore, life-sustaining treatments can also include medications that support essential bodily functions, such as medication for high blood pressure or diabetes.

Living will: An advance medical directive that specifies what types of medical treatment are desired. A living will can be very specific or very general. The most common statement in a living will requests that if the patient suffers an incurable, irreversible illness.

Mechanical ventilation: The tube is actually inserted through the mouth or nose and down into the trachea (windpipe), not the esophagus as previously stated.

Mechanical ventilation is a medical treatment that is used to support or replace the function of the lungs. A machine called a ventilator (or respirator) is used to force air into the lungs. The ventilator is attached to a tube that is inserted through the mouth or nose and down into the trachea (windpipe). The tube is then connected to the ventilator, which pumps air into the lungs and helps the patient breathe. Mechanical ventilation may be used for a variety of conditions, including respiratory failure, severe lung infections, or after certain surgeries.

Medical power of attorney: Medical power of attorney is a legal document that allows individuals to appoint someone else to make healthcare decisions on their behalf if they are unable to do so themselves. The appointed person is known as a healthcare agent, surrogate, attorney-in-fact, or proxy, and is responsible for ensuring that the patient's wishes are respected and followed.

Medicare: The US government's national health insurance program for people aged 65 and older who have worked for at least 10 years in Medicare-covered employment, and who are citizens or permanent residents of the US. Medicare Part A covers inpatient hospital stays, and Medicare Part B covers physician and outpatient services. Furthermore, Medicare Part C, also known as Medicare Advantage, is an optional plan that provides coverage through private insurance companies. Medicare Part D provides prescription drug coverage.

Metastasis: Metastasis is the spread of cancer cells from the original site to distant parts of the body through the bloodstream or lymphatic system. This is a critical factor in determining the stage of cancer and the appropriate course of treatment.

Morality Rate: The term "mortality rate", is the number of deaths in a population during a specific period of time (usually a year) divided by the total number of people in the population. It is usually expressed as a rate per 1,000 or 100,000 people.

Morphine: A powerful narcotic agent that has strong analgesic (pain relief) action and other significant effects on the central nervous system. It is dangerously addicting. Morphine is a naturally occurring member of a large chemical class of compounds called alkaloids. The name derives from Morpheus (the Greek god of dreams), not the Roman god.
, was coined in 1805 by German apothecary Adolf Serturner to designate the main alkaloid in opium. Opium comes from the poppy plant.

Music therapy: Music therapy is a healthcare profession that uses music to address the physical, emotional, cognitive, and social needs of individuals of all ages. A trained music therapist uses music interventions that are designed to support the individual's specific needs and goals. Music therapy can help individuals with a variety of conditions including but not limited to physical disabilities, mental health disorders, chronic pain, developmental and learning disabilities, and neurological disorders. The interventions can include creating, singing, moving to, and/or listening to music, and can be provided in individual or group settings.

Narcotics: Narcotics, also known as opioids, are a class of drugs that are used to treat pain. They work by binding to receptors in the brain and spinal cord, which can lead to pain relief as well as sedation and euphoria. Some common examples of narcotics include morphine, oxycodone, hydrocodone, fentanyl, and heroin. Narcotics can be highly addictive and have a high potential for abuse and overdose. They are typically prescribed by a doctor and should be used only as directed.

Nausea: Stomach queasiness, the urge to vomit. Nausea can be brought on by many causes, including systemic illnesses (such as influenza), medications, pain, and inner ear disease. In addition, nausea is also a common symptom of pregnancy, motion sickness, chemotherapy, and certain medical conditions such as gastroesophageal reflux disease (GERD) and peptic ulcers. It can be accompanied by other symptoms such as sweating, dizziness, and an increased heart rate.

Nurse: 1) A person trained, licensed, or skilled in nursing. 2) To feed an infant at the breast.

Nursing: 1) Profession concerned with the provision of services essential to the maintenance and restoration of health by attending the needs of sick persons. 2) Feeding an infant at the breast.

Nursing home: A residential facility for people with chronic illness or disability, particularly older people who have mobility and eating problems. Also known as a convalescent home and long-term care facility. Just a minor correction - while nursing homes can certainly provide care for people with chronic illness or disability, they are not necessarily limited to older people. People of all ages may live in nursing homes if they require long-term care due to a medical condition or disability.

Nutritionist: 1) In a hospital or nursing home, a person who plans and/or formulates special meals for patients. It can also simply be a euphemism for a cook who works in a medical facility but who does not have extensive training in special nutritional needs. 2) In clinical practice, a specialist in nutrition. Nutritionists can help patients with special needs, allergies, health problems, or a desire for increased energy or weight change devise healthy diets. Some nutritionists in private practice are well- trained, hold a degree and are licensed. Depending on state law, however, a person using the title may not be trained or licensed at all. That's correct! However, I would like to add that in some states, the title "nutritionist" is legally protected and can only be used by individuals who meet certain educational and professional requirements, such as holding a degree in nutrition and passing a certification exam. In other states, the title may not be protected and can be used by anyone, regardless of their qualifications. To ensure that you are receiving advice from a qualified professional, it is recommended to look for a registered dietitian nutritionist (RDN) who has met the rigorous educational and professional requirements set by the Academy of Nutrition and Dietetics.

Opioid: 1. a synthetic narcotic that resembles the naturally occurring opiates. 2. Any substance that binds to or otherwise affects the opiate receptors on the surface of the cell. Just a small correction, opioids are not necessarily synthetic, they can also be naturally occurring.

The definition of opioid is: any substance, natural or synthetic, that binds to the opioid receptors in the brain and other parts of the body, producing effects such as pain relief, sedation, and euphoria.

Pain: An unpleasant sensation that can range from mild, localized discomfort to agony. Pain has both physical and emotional components. The physical part of pain results from nerve stimulation. Pain may be contained to a discrete area, as in an injury, or it can be more diffuse, as in disorders like fibromyalgia. Pain is mediated by specific nerve fibers that carry the pain impulses to the brain where their conscious appreciation may be modified by many factors. To In addition, pain can be acute or chronic. Acute pain is a sudden, sharp or severe pain that lasts for a short period and is usually caused by an injury or illness. Chronic pain, on the other hand, lasts for longer periods, often over 3-6 months, and may not have an obvious cause. Chronic pain can be very debilitating and may affect a person's physical and emotional well-being.

Palliation: therapy designed to relieve uncomfortable symptoms without producing a cure. Yes, that is correct. Palliative care is a type of medical care that focuses on providing relief from symptoms and improving the quality of life for patients with serious or life-threatening illnesses. The goal of palliative care is not to cure the underlying disease, but to manage symptoms such as pain, nausea, and difficulty breathing, and to address the psychological, social, and spiritual needs of the patient and their family. Palliative care can be provided alongside other medical treatments and may be appropriate at any stage of an illness, from diagnosis to end-of-life care.

Palliative care: 1) Medical or comfort care that reduces the severity of a disease or slows its progress rather than providing a cure. For incurable diseases, in cases where the cure is not recommended due to other health concerns, and when the patient does not wish to pursue a cure, palliative care becomes the focus of treatment. For example, if surgery cannot be performed to remove a tumor, radiation treatment might be tried to reduce its rate of growth, and pain management could help the patient manage physical symptoms. 2) In a negative sense, provision only of perfunctory health care when a cure is possible. To clarify, the second part of the definition "in a negative sense, the provision only of perfunctory health care when a cure is possible" is not an accurate description of palliative care. Palliative care is focused on providing comprehensive care to manage symptoms, improve quality of life, and address the emotional and spiritual needs of patients with serious or life-limiting illnesses. It is not intended to replace curative treatments, but rather to be integrated alongside them to provide holistic care.

Patient Caregiver: a person who agrees to take responsibility for the 24-hour care of hospice patients, either personally or with assistance. In the context of hospice care, a patient caregiver refers to a family member, friend, or other individual who agrees to provide care and support to a hospice patient on a daily basis. This can include assistance with activities of daily living, emotional support, and help with medical needs such as administering medication. The patient caregiver may work alongside a hospice team including nurses, social workers, and other healthcare professionals to ensure the patient's comfort and well-being.

Pediatrics: The field of medicine that is concerned with the health of infants, children, and adolescents; their growth and development; and their opportunity to achieve full potential as adults. That's correct! Pediatrics is a branch of medicine that deals with the medical care of infants, children, and adolescents up to the age of 18. Pediatricians are specialized doctors who provide medical care to children and adolescents, including diagnosis and treatment of illnesses, injuries, and disorders. They also monitor growth and development, provide guidance on nutrition and physical activity, and work with families to promote the health and well-being of children.

Pharmacy: A location where prescription medications are sold. A pharmacy is constantly supervised by a licensed pharmacist. To add to that, a pharmacy is also responsible for dispensing medications, providing information about medications to patients and healthcare professionals, monitoring medication use and interactions, and ensuring the safe storage and disposal of medications. Pharmacies may also sell over-the-counter medications, medical supplies, and other healthcare-related products. In addition to community pharmacies, there are also hospital pharmacies, compounding pharmacies, and mail-order pharmacies.

Prognosis: Prognosis is an estimate of the probable course and outcome of a disease, especially the chances of recovery, based on available clinical, laboratory, and radiological data, as well as the person's medical history and other factors that may affect the disease's progression. Prognosis can be used to guide treatment decisions, inform patients and their families about the potential risks and benefits of different therapies, and help healthcare providers anticipate and manage potential complications.

Quality of life: The patient's ability to enjoy normal life activities. Quality of life is an important consideration in medical care. Some medical treatments can seriously impair the quality of life without providing appreciable benefits, whereas others greatly enhance the quality of life. To add to that, Quality of Life (QoL) is a multidimensional concept that includes various aspects such as physical, emotional, social, and spiritual well-being. It refers to the overall satisfaction and happiness that a person experiences in their daily life. In the medical context, QoL is often used to assess the impact of a disease, disorder, or treatment on a patient's well-being. It is important to consider QoL when making decisions about medical interventions, especially in cases where the intervention may have significant side effects or risks.

Radiation: Radiation therapy is a type of cancer treatment that uses high-energy radiation to shrink tumors and kill cancer cells. The radiation can come from a machine outside the body (external-beam radiation therapy), or it can be delivered internally, by placing radioactive material inside the body (brachytherapy). Radiation therapy is designed to damage the DNA of cancer cells, which inhibits their ability to divide and grow. While radiation therapy can cause some damage to healthy cells, the goal is to limit that damage as much as possible while still effectively treating the cancer.

Remission: Remission refers to the period during which the symptoms of a disease are reduced or disappear altogether. It is often used in the context of cancer and other chronic diseases such as multiple sclerosis, lupus, and rheumatoid arthritis. A remission can be partial or complete, and it may be temporary or permanent. The term "remission" is often used interchangeably with "response" when describing the effect of a particular treatment on a disease.

Respiratory arrest: Respiratory arrest is the cessation of breathing. It can lead to cardiac arrest if not promptly treated. Thank you for bringing it to my attention.

Respite: Respite can refer to a temporary break or relief from a stressful situation, often used in the context of caregiving. For example, a caregiver of a terminally ill patient may need respite care to take a break from the demands of caregiving and to prevent burnout. Respite care can involve having someone else take over caregiving duties temporarily or having the patient stay in a facility for a short period of time.

Sleep: Sleep is a naturally recurring state of mind and body characterized by altered consciousness, reduced muscle activity, and limited responsiveness to external stimuli. During sleep, the body undergoes a number of physiological processes including repair and rejuvenation of cells, consolidation of memory, and regulation of hormones. The quality and quantity of sleep can have a significant impact on physical and mental health, and inadequate sleep has been linked to a variety of health problems.

Social Death: Social death, also known as social dying or social exclusion, refers to the phenomenon of people avoiding or ostracizing a dying person. It can occur for a variety of reasons, including fear of contagion, discomfort with the dying process, or cultural taboos surrounding death and dying.

Social death can have a significant impact on the dying person's mental and emotional well-being, as they may feel isolated and abandoned during a time when they most need support and companionship. It can also lead to feelings of shame and guilt for the individuals who are avoiding the dying person.

It is important to recognize and address social death to ensure that dying individuals are treated with dignity and respect and that they have access to the care and support they need during their final days. This can include providing education and resources to help people understand and overcome their fears and discomfort surrounding death, as well as fostering a culture of openness and compassion around end-of-life issues.

Sublingual: Rublingual refers to a method of medication delivery in which the medication is placed under the tongue and allowed to dissolve or be absorbed by the tissues in the mouth. Sublingual medications are typically in the form of tablets, films, or sprays and are designed to be quickly absorbed into the bloodstream through the thin tissues under the tongue.

This method of medication delivery is often used when a medication needs to be rapidly absorbed into the bloodstream or when it is destroyed by the digestive system if taken orally. Sublingual medications can be used to treat a variety of conditions, including angina, allergies, and certain types of pain.

It is important to follow the instructions for taking sublingual medications carefully, as they may have specific dosing and administration requirements. It is also important to be aware of any potential side effects or interactions with other medications that may occur when taking a sublingual medication.

Surrogate decision-making: Surrogate decision-making refers to a legal process in which a group of individuals, typically family members, are authorized to make decisions about medical treatments on behalf of a patient who has lost decision-making capacity and did not prepare an advance directive.

In the United States, a majority of states have passed laws that permit surrogate decision-making for people without advance directives. These laws typically establish a hierarchy of individuals who are authorized to make decisions on behalf of the patient, starting with a spouse, then adult children, parents, siblings, and other relatives. In some cases, close friends or legal guardians may also be authorized to make decisions.

Surrogate decision-making can be a complex and emotionally challenging process, as it often involves difficult decisions about end-of-life care and treatment options. It is important for the surrogate decision-makers to work closely with healthcare providers to ensure that they understand the patient's medical condition, prognosis, and treatment options, and to make decisions that are consistent with the patient's values and preferences.

It is also important for individuals to prepare advance directives, such as a living will or durable power of attorney for healthcare, to provide guidance about their medical treatment preferences in the event that they are unable to make decisions for themselves. This can help to ensure that their wishes are respected and that their loved ones are not burdened with the responsibility of making difficult decisions without guidance.

Syndrome: A syndrome is a collection of symptoms and signs that tend to occur together and are indicative of a particular medical condition or disease. Syndromes can be caused by a variety of factors, including genetic mutations, infections, environmental factors, and other underlying medical conditions.

A syndrome may have a wide range of symptoms and severity, and some may be associated with a specific set of physical characteristics or traits. Examples of syndromes include Down syndrome, which is characterized by intellectual disability, distinctive facial features, and certain physical abnormalities; Asperger syndrome, which is characterized by social and communication difficulties, as well as repetitive behaviors and interests; and Tourette syndrome, which is characterized by involuntary movements and vocalizations, called tics.

The diagnosis of a syndrome typically involves a thorough evaluation of the patient's medical history, physical examination, and often, laboratory or imaging tests. Treatment for a syndrome depends on the underlying cause and symptoms, and may include medication, therapy, surgery, or other interventions.

It is important to note that not all symptoms or groups of symptoms are classified as a syndrome, as the term refers specifically to a set of symptoms that are recognized as being associated with a particular medical condition or disease.

Taste: A perception that results from stimulation of a gustatory nerve. Taste belongs to the chemical sensing system. Tasting begins when molecules stimulate special cells in the mouth or throat. These special cells transmit messages through nerves to the brain, where specific tastes are identified. Gustatory, or taste, cells react to food and beverages. The taste cells are clustered in the taste buds of the mouth and throat. Many of the small bumps that can be seen on the tongue contain taste buds. Smell contributes to the sense of taste, as does another chemosensory mechanism, called the common chemical sense. In this system, thousands of nerve endings, especially on the moist surfaces of the eyes, nose, mouth, and throat, give rise to sensations such as the sting of ammonia, the coolness of menthol, and the irritation of chili peppers. People can commonly identify four basic taste sensations: sweet, sour, bitter, and salty. In the mouth, these tastes, along with texture, temperature, and sensations from the common chemical sense, combine with odors to produce the perception of flavor. Flavors are recognized mainly through the sense of smell. If a person holds his or her nose while eating chocolate, for example, the person will have trouble identifying the chocolate flavor even though he or she can distinguish the food's sweetness or bitterness. That is because the familiar flavor of chocolate is sensed largely by odor.

Terminal: The term "terminal" refers to the final stages of a disease or condition that is likely to result in death. This can include a wide range of conditions, such as advanced cancer, heart failure, chronic obstructive pulmonary disease (COPD), or Alzheimer's disease, among others.

In the terminal stage of a disease, the patient's condition may be characterized by a significant decline in physical and mental functioning, as well as increased pain, discomfort, and other symptoms. Treatment during this stage often focuses on providing comfort and palliative care to improve the patient's quality of life and manage symptoms such as pain, nausea, and shortness of breath.

For patients and their families, the terminal stage of a disease can be an emotionally challenging time and may involve difficult decisions about end-of-life care and treatment options. In some cases, patients may choose to forgo certain treatments in order to focus on the quality of life and make the most of the time they have left.

It is important for patients and their families to work closely with healthcare providers during the terminal stage of a disease to ensure that their wishes and preferences are respected, and to ensure that they receive appropriate care and support during this difficult time.

Thanatology: Thanatology is the scientific study of death, dying, and the bereavement process. It is a multidisciplinary field that draws on insights and research from a variety of fields, including psychology, sociology, anthropology, medicine, ethics, philosophy, and religion.

The study of thanatology encompasses a wide range of topics, including the biological, psychological, social, and cultural aspects of death and dying, as well as the experiences of individuals who are facing death, their families, and their caregivers. It also includes the study of grief and bereavement, and the various ways in which individuals and communities cope with loss and the end of life.

Some of the key areas of research within thanatology include the factors that influence attitudes and beliefs about death and dying, the psychological and emotional experiences of individuals who are facing death or caring for those who are dying, the social and cultural aspects of end-of-life care, and the ethical and legal issues that arise in the context of death and dying.

Thanatology has important implications for the practice of healthcare and for the development of policies and programs related to end-of-life care. It can help to inform the development of interventions and resources that support patients and families during the dying process and the bereavement process and can also help to promote greater understanding and acceptance of death as a natural and inevitable part of the human experience.

Therapy: While therapy can be a form of treatment for disease, it is not always synonymous with treatment. Therapy refers to a broad range of interventions and techniques aimed at promoting health and well-being, preventing and treating illness or injury, and addressing emotional, behavioral, or cognitive issues.

Therapy can encompass a wide range of modalities, including medication, psychotherapy, physical therapy, occupational therapy, speech therapy, and more. Each type of therapy is designed to address specific needs and challenges and may involve different techniques and approaches.

For example, psychotherapy is a type of therapy that focuses on addressing mental and emotional health issues, such as anxiety, depression, and post-traumatic stress disorder (PTSD). It often involves talking with a trained mental health professional and may involve techniques such as cognitive-behavioral therapy, psychodynamic therapy, or interpersonal therapy.

Physical therapy, on the other hand, is a type of therapy that focuses on restoring function and mobility to the body after injury or illness. It often involves exercises, stretches, and other techniques aimed at improving strength, flexibility, and range of motion.

While therapy can certainly be a form of treatment for disease or illness, it is important to note that not all forms of therapy are aimed at treating a specific disease or condition. Some forms of therapy are focused on promoting general health and well-being, improving quality of life, or addressing specific challenges or goals.

Withholding or withdrawing treatment: Withholding or withdrawing treatment refers to the decision to forgo or discontinue life-sustaining measures that have been used to treat a patient with a serious or terminal illness. This decision may be made by the patient or their family, in consultation with healthcare providers, and is typically based on the patient's wishes, prognosis, and overall quality of life.

Life-sustaining measures can include a wide range of interventions, such as mechanical ventilation, artificial nutrition and hydration, and cardiopulmonary resuscitation (CPR). These interventions may be necessary to keep a patient alive, but they can also be invasive, and uncomfortable, and may not always be effective in prolonging life or improving quality of life.

Withholding or withdrawing treatment is often considered to be an ethical and legal issue, and there are specific guidelines and protocols that healthcare providers must follow when making these decisions. In many cases, the decision to forgo or discontinue life-sustaining measures is made in accordance with the patient's advance directives, such as a living will or a durable power of attorney for healthcare.

In cases where the patient has not made their wishes known, healthcare providers may consult with the patient's family or other surrogate decision-makers to determine the most appropriate course of action. The decision to withhold or withdraw treatment should always be made with the patient's best interests in mind and should take into account their values, beliefs, and overall quality of life.

STAGES OF DYING

The physical aspect of dying refers to the final stages of the dying process, during which the body's systems gradually shut down and cease to function. This process can be divided into several stages, including the following:

1. The pre-active stage: During this stage, the person may experience changes in breathing, blood pressure, and body temperature, as well as other physical and emotional symptoms.

2. The active stage: This stage is characterized by a rapid decline in the person's physical condition, including changes in breathing and heart rate, decreased consciousness, and other symptoms such as restlessness, agitation, or confusion.

3. The terminal stage: This is the final stage of the dying process, during which the person's body shuts down completely and physical systems cease to function. This can include the cessation of breathing, heart rate, and other vital signs.

The physical aspect of dying can be a difficult and distressing experience for both the dying person and their loved ones. However, there are often ways to manage symptoms and provide comfort and support during this process. Hospice and palliative care teams, for example, are trained to provide comprehensive care and support to individuals who are nearing the end of life, with a focus on managing pain and other physical symptoms, as well as addressing emotional, social, and spiritual needs.

The other dynamic is the emotional/mental/spiritual area which is a different process. This is where the spirit of the dying individual begins to slip away from its immediate environment and attachments. This release tends to follow its own priorities when it comes to letting go of loved ones and unfinished business. You have all heard people tell how someone on their deathbed refuses to let go until a certain member of the family is able to get there. Even when the body is trying to shut down the spirit hangs on until a resolution is reached. It is as though those dying need permission to go and to feel that they have achieved the support and acceptance of their fate from the people they will leave behind. This way, they can slip into the next dimension of life with grace and dignity.

There is in all of us a curiosity about dying. Regardless of your religious beliefs, there has to be some doubt or shadows of uncertainty. There are five stages involved. Some patients have time to experience each stage and come to a peaceful resolution. Each person approaches death in their own way, bringing to their individual process uniqueness. Death comes in its own time and in its own way. It is as unique as the individual experiencing it.

FIVE STAGES OF DYING

The five stages of dying, also known as the Kübler-Ross model, are a series of emotional and psychological stages that are often experienced by individuals who are facing death or a serious illness. The stages were first identified by Swiss-American psychiatrist Elisabeth Kübler-Ross in her book "On Death and Dying" in 1969.

The five stages are as follows:

1. Denial: In the first stage, the individual may experience shock and disbelief, and may deny the reality of the situation. They may refuse to acknowledge that they are dying, and may resist any attempts to discuss their condition.

2. Anger: In the second stage, the individual may experience feelings of anger, resentment, or bitterness. They may feel that their illness or impending death is unfair, and may direct their anger towards loved ones, healthcare providers, or even a higher power.

3. Bargaining: In the third stage, the individual may attempt to negotiate with themselves, others, or a higher power in an attempt to avoid death. They may make promises or ask for more time, and may try to find a sense of meaning or purpose in their life.

4. Depression: In the fourth stage, the individual may experience feelings of sadness, hopelessness, and despair. They may feel overwhelmed by their situation, and may withdraw from others or lose interest in the world around them.

5. Acceptance: In the final stage, the individual comes to terms with their situation and begins to accept the reality of their impending death. They may experience a sense of peace, and may focus on making the most of the time they have left.

It's important to note that not everyone experiences all five stages and that the stages may not necessarily occur in a linear or predictable order. Additionally, the stages may be experienced differently by individuals from different cultural or religious backgrounds, and the experience of dying can be influenced by a wide range of factors, including the individual's physical condition, social support, and personal beliefs.

DENIAL: Patients think, "I'm too young to die. I'm not ready to die." (Is anyone really ever ready? Does someone just get up some morning and say, "Well, I'm ready to die today?") Even when a physician informs someone that nothing can be done for them, the feeling that some mistake must have been made is in the dying person's mind. The prediction from a physician of imminent death can do several things. It can give patients time to prepare, take care of business, close doors, and/or make amends. The shock begins to ebb as they come to grips with approaching death.

ANGER: Suddenly patients have no control over life or death. They have no choice … they are going to die. They have always known that death is a part of life but now it's a fact directly before them. It makes them angry. They feel so helpless, especially at first, then guilt climbs upon them and anger is directed at everyone and no one in particular. It is a sense of loss of control which is likely not a new feeling if the patient has endured a long illness. It is normal. Anger is, on its own, a sense of strength. However, it can also be debilitating.

BARGAINING: Patients are now willing to compromise. No use denying it, anger comes and goes so perhaps they can make a deal with God! They are willing to promise to do, or not to do, specific things if only they can be given more time. It can be based on an upcoming event that is important to them. They can be suffering from insecurities regarding members of the family or a loved one whom they feel is dependent on them. There can be a rift that has never been eliminated that needs to be further addressed. They are not free to go until these open items can be completed once and for all.

DEPRESSION: This is such a normal part of the process of preparing to die. Patients are already depressed about their incapability to deal with certain responsibilities, projects, and tasks of everyday life. Symptoms of terminal illness are impossible to ignore and patients are fully aware that death is inevitable. Aware, angry, and filled with sorrow, again the culprit of guilt sneaks in as patients mourn for themselves and the pain that this is causing their loved ones. Again, depression is a totally normal phase in the dying process.

ACCEPTANCE: This comes after patients work through the numerous conflicts and feelings that dying brings. They can succumb to the inevitable as they become more tired and weakness hangs on. Patients become less emotional; calmness arrives and banishes fear just as joy conquers sadness. They realize the battle is almost over and now it's right for them to die.

HOW THE BODY PREPARES FOR THE ONSET OF DYING

The body goes through several changes as it prepares for the onset of dying. These changes can vary depending on the individual and the underlying cause of their illness or condition. Some of the common changes that occur include:

1. Loss of appetite and decreased fluid intake: As the body begins to shut down, the individual may lose their appetite and may not feel like eating or drinking. This can lead to dehydration and malnutrition and can cause further deterioration in the individual's physical condition.
2. Changes in breathing: The individual's breathing may become irregular or labored, and they may experience shortness of breath or gasping for air. They may also develop a rattling sound in their chest, known as the death rattle, which is caused by the accumulation of mucus in the airways.
3. Changes in circulation: The individual's circulation may become compromised, leading to a drop in blood pressure, cold extremities, and a weakened pulse.

4. Changes in consciousness: The individual may become less responsive or may slip into a coma-like state. They may also experience hallucinations or delirium.
5. Changes in skin color and temperature: The individual's skin may become cool to the touch and may take on a bluish or grayish tint. This is due to a decrease in blood flow and oxygenation.

It's important to note that these changes do not necessarily occur in a predictable or linear fashion and that the timing and extent of these changes can vary widely depending on the individual's underlying condition. Additionally, the experience of dying can be influenced by a wide range of factors, including the individual's personal beliefs, social support, and cultural or religious background.

There are many different ways the body prepares for the onset of dying and they all seem to show one thing, the body starts shutting down one system after the other.

Here are some signs of how the body prepares for the onset of dying:

> The first thing that you might notice is a person's hands and feet become extremely cold. In addition, the skin color changes with it being mottled; this is a clear indication that the circulation of blood to the extremities has decreased and only the vital organs are being supplied with blood.

> A person who is about to die tends to sleep a lot. This is no ordinary sleep but rather, it is a deep and sound sleep where you will find it difficult to wake up the person.

> Disorientation is common in people who are about to die. They seem confused and cannot identify their surroundings or the people around them.

> Incontinence is a common sign of how the body prepares for the unset of dying. A person who is about to die can lose control over his bladder and/or bowels.

> A decrease in food and fluid intake is another sign of how the body prepares to die. The person will not feel hungry or thirsty and it is best not to force them as it will make them uncomfortable. Due to lack of fluid urination will become infrequent and concentrated.

> The breathing pattern becomes shallow and there is a big gap between two breaths (chain stoking).

> A death rattle is a gurgling or rattle-like noise produced shortly before death by the accumulation of excessive respiratory secretions in the throat. The death rattle is a clear indication that someone is near death.

Working through the Pain of Losing a loved one

Losing a loved one can be an incredibly difficult and painful experience, and it's normal to feel a wide range of emotions during the grieving process. Here are some strategies that can help individuals work through the pain of losing a loved one:

1. Allow yourself to grieve: It's important to give yourself permission to feel the pain of your loss, and to allow yourself to grieve in your own way and at your own pace. This may involve crying, talking about your feelings, or engaging in activities that bring you comfort or solace.

2. Seek support: It can be helpful to reach out to friends, family members, or a support group for help and support during this difficult time. Talking to others who have experienced a similar loss can help you feel less alone, and can provide valuable insight and perspective.

3. Take care of yourself: It's important to take care of your physical and emotional health during the grieving process. This may involve eating healthy foods, getting enough rest, exercising regularly, and engaging in activities that bring you joy or relaxation.

4. Express your feelings: Whether through writing, art, or other creative outlets, expressing your feelings can be a helpful way to process your emotions and work through the pain of your loss.

5. Find meaning: Finding meaning in your loss can be an important part of the grieving process. This may involve finding ways to honor your loved one's memory, engaging in activities that they enjoyed, or finding ways to make a positive impact in the world in their name.

It's important to remember that the grieving process is unique to each individual and that there is no "right" way to grieve. It's okay to feel a wide range of emotions and to take the time you need to heal and work through the pain of your loss. If you're struggling to cope with your grief, it may be helpful to seek professional support from a therapist or counselor.

Understanding Loss examines the ways that loss is wound.

Natures Anesthetic takes a closer look at shock and denial and how to cope.

The Many Faces of Anger reveals the necessity of the anger phase of grief and how to make this stage of the healing process work for the griever in positive ways.

Making a Deal with God explores the bargaining phase for grief and the opportunities it offers for personal growth and greater healing.

In the Valley of the Shadow reveals how to gain strength and perspective from the depression stage in the grief process

The Ravages of Remorse deals with guilt feelings and the crippling effects they can have on the healing process.

Return to Sunshine shows how to nurture hope and find renewal in the acceptance phase of grief.

The process of grieving cannot be hurried. It takes a great deal of time usually a year or more. It may be the purest pain one can ever know. The following are stages of grief commonly experienced. You may not experience all of these, and you may not experience them in this order. It is important to realize, however, that what you are feeling is NATURAL; and you will begin to heal. Shock: feeling numb, no display of fear or emotions.

Emotional Release: at some point beginning to feel pain and hurt.

Preoccupation: difficulty thinking of other things.

Physical and Emotional Distress: sleeplessness, tightness in the throat, choking feeling, shortness of breath, sighing, an empty, hollow feeling in the stomach, lack of muscular power, digestive symptoms, poor appetite, a slight sense of unreality, emotional distance, panic, and thoughts of self-destruction.

Hostile Reactions: display of unwarranted hostility.

Guilt: A sense of being responsible for not taking action to prevent the situation.

Depression: feelings of despair, unbearable loneliness, and hopelessness.

Withdrawal: withdrawing from social relationships.

Reentering Relationships: After a period of time the grieving person reestablishes old relationships and begins to form new ones.

Resolution and Readjustment: This comes gradually; the memories are still there; the love is still there; and healing begins.

COMMON RESPONSES TO GRIEF

Grief is a complex and individual experience, and people can respond to it in different ways. However, there are some common responses to grief that many people experience. Here are a few:

1. Denial: In the early stages of grief, it's common to feel a sense of disbelief or denial about the loss. This may involve feeling like the person is still alive or expecting them to come back.
2. Anger: It's also common to feel angry in response to a loss. This may involve feeling angry at the person who died, at oneself, at others, or at the situation itself.
3. Bargaining: Some people may try to bargain with a higher power or with themselves in an attempt to undo the loss or make it less painful.
4. Depression: Grief can also lead to feelings of sadness, hopelessness, and despair. These feelings can be intense and long-lasting and can interfere with daily functioning.
5. Acceptance: Over time, many people can come to a place of acceptance about the loss. This doesn't mean that they no longer feel sadness or pain, but rather that they have found a way to live with it and integrate it into their lives.

It's important to note that these responses to grief can vary widely depending on the individual and their personal experience. Additionally, there is no "right" way to grieve, and people may experience different emotions or responses at different times during the grieving process.

You will note that the common responses to grief closely resemble the responses to the dying process:

> A feeling of tightness in the throat or heaviness in the chest.

> An empty feeling in the stomach and loss of appetite.
> Restlessness and a need for activity, accompanied by the inability to concentrate.
> A feeling that loss isn't real, that it didn't really happen.
> A sense of your lost one's presence, like finding yourself expecting them to walk in the door, hearing their voice, or seeing their face.
> Aimless wandering, forgetfulness, and inability to finish things you've started to do around the house.
> Difficulty sleeping, frequent dreams about the incident or related incidences.
> A tendency to assume the mannerisms or traits of your deceased loved one.
> Intense anger at your loved one for leaving you.
> An intense preoccupation with the life of your deceased loved one.
> A need to take care of other people around you.
> A need to tell, re-tell, and remember things about the deceased or the incident.
> Crying at unexpected times.

These are all-natural and normal grief responses. It is important to cry and talk with people when you need to.

SUPPORT STRATEGIES

"The first question which the priest and the Levite asked was:

'If I stop to help this man, what will happen to me?'

But…the Good Samaritan reversed the question:

'If I do not stop to help this man, what will happen to him?'

Martin Luther King Jr.

Helping Others (Do's and Don'ts):

DO…

- ✓ Pray continually, for the person and for your conversation and contacts, that you may be a healing agent by the Holy Spirit.
- ✓ Be present with the person. Make yourself available and let the person know you are there simply because you care.
- ✓ Meet practical needs. It's good to offer and provide groceries or other items, but be sensitive to what they actually need.
- ✓ Accept and validate the feelings expressed. They are their true feelings, even if they are directed at God or seem to be a crisis of faith. Problems, attitudes, and issues can be dealt with in time.
- ✓ Be there long term. Let others know you care and allow them to set the pace of discussions and relationships.
- ✓ Let them question God and spiritual things. It is okay, to say you don't agree with a statement they make in anger, as long as you limit it to your view and don't try to "correct" their view of God theologically at this point.
- ✓ Use a comforting touch. A hug or a pat on the shoulder does help.
- ✓ Avoid curiosity. Inappropriate details of crime.
- ✓ Listen to what others mean, not just what they say.
- ✓ Be sensitive to their emotional needs when you speak.
- ✓ Use a sense of humor when it is appropriate.
- ✓ Take care of yourself by time off and seeking support from others.
- ✓ Use creative arts to help others express their feeling (poetry, songs, etc.)
- ✓ Find scriptures to share. The word used sensitively, wisely, and appropriately will deal with others where they are.

✓   Understand your role in the healing process. See the Good Samaritan passage (Luke 10:25-37).

DON'T…

✗   Blame the victim. Avoid questions or statements that point to "contributing factors" of the situation.

✗   Assume you know how to define forgiveness. It is not forgetting as we are consistently told.

✗   Rush forgiveness. Forgiveness is commanded by God but rushing it may be misconstrued as manipulating the situation.

✗   Use Clichés. Packaged statements only make the caregiver feel good, and they belittle the others.

✗   Place expectations of any kind. Quite often survivors need to have a sense of recovering their own ability to cope with life and even daily things. Placing expectations on them robs them of the power to cope.

✗   Intellectualize or theologize their situation. Neither will help emotional or spiritual growth. Most of the time intellectual or theological statements are not as objective as they may have been intended to be.

✗   Expect grief to be an easy step by step process. Grief works differently for different situations and for different people. There may be characteristics that we should understand but no one will go through them exactly the same as another.

✗   Distance or isolate the others. It is our natural tendency to pull away from those whom have gone through something horrific or something we don't understand. Draw near to them as a friend.

✗   Get too close. It is easy to become over involved in someone's emotional state, or feel like you have to be sharing their pain for yourself in order to help them.

- ✗   Say you understand. No one understands the uniqueness of another's pain or circumstance. Try to understand but don't pretend that you do.
- ✗   Over busy others. It is easy for us to busy ourselves to forget pain, but that doesn't deal with it. Keep them busy enough to feel like a part of the community, but let them rest and process with you on the down days as well.

Pass info on. Ask permission for what you can share with others, and what attention the survivor desires.

DEATH AND CULTURAL GENERALITIES

Death is a universal experience, but cultural attitudes and beliefs about death can vary widely. Here are a few cultural generalities related to death:

1. Beliefs about the afterlife: Many cultures have beliefs about what happens to the soul or spirit after death. Some believe in an afterlife, while others believe in reincarnation or that the spirit lives on in some other form.

2. Funeral rituals: Funerals and other death rituals can vary widely between cultures. Some cultures have elaborated funeral rituals that involve specific clothing, music, or decorations, while others have simpler or more private rituals.

3. Mourning practices: Mourning practices can also vary widely between cultures. Some cultures have specific mourning periods or rituals, while others may not have formalized mourning practices.

4. Beliefs about death and dying: Cultural beliefs about death and dying can also vary widely. Some cultures may view death as a natural part of life, while others may view it as a taboo subject.

5. Treatment of the deceased: The treatment of the deceased can also vary between cultures. Some cultures may bury or cremate the deceased, while others may practice sky burials or other methods.

It's important to note that these are generalities and that individual attitudes and beliefs can vary widely even within a culture.

Additionally, cultural attitudes and beliefs about death can change over time.

The following general statements outline some of the ethnic cultures surrounding death:

Hispanic tradition tends to support family and friends, including children. Time is spent with the deceased before burial. Touching, dressing, and arranging are normal. Outward expressions of grief are common including crying and sometimes fainting. There is a lot of activity and it includes all ages. Promises are made to the deceased, which are usually honored. Yes, that is correct. In many Hispanic cultures, family, and community are very important, and this extends to the way that death is approached and processed. Traditionally, family and friends will spend time with the deceased before burial, touching and arranging the body as a way of saying goodbye. Outward expressions of grief, including crying and fainting, are often seen as natural and acceptable ways of expressing emotions. In some Hispanic cultures, there may be a lot of activity surrounding death and mourning, and people of all ages may be involved in the process. Additionally, it is common to make promises to the deceased, such as promising to carry on their legacy or to take care of loved ones, and these promises are often taken very seriously and honored by the community.

African Influences cover a wide range of traditions and span many generations. Generally, there is a support system of family and friends. Immediately after death, close friends and members of the family usually gather at the home of the deceased to offer condolences and comfort the next of kin. Recent immigrants tend to have more open expressions of grief than people with longer American heritage. However, in many African cultures, family and community are very important and this extends to the way that death is approached and processed.

Immediately after death, it is common for close friends and family members to gather at the home of the deceased to offer condolences and support to the next of kin. This can include traditional mourning practices such as singing, dancing, and sharing stories about the deceased. In some African cultures, it is also common for people to wear specific clothing or jewelry as a sign of mourning.

Recent immigrants to the United States may have more open expressions of grief and may continue to practice traditional mourning rituals, while those with longer American heritage may have adapted to more Westernized mourning practices. It's important to note that these are generalities and that individual attitudes and beliefs can vary widely even within a cultural group.

Asian Communities have a wide variety of death and mourning traditions that can vary greatly depending on the specific culture and religion. However, there are some common themes that are seen across many Asian traditions.

Respect for the deceased and their well-being is a fundamental aspect of many Asian cultures. In some cultures, it is traditional to keep the body of the deceased at home for several days after death, and family members may offer food and incense to the deceased as a sign of respect. It is also common for family members to participate in preparing the body for burial or cremation, including washing and dressing the body.

In many Asian cultures, there are specific mourning rituals that are followed in the days or weeks after a death, such as wearing specific clothing or jewelry, refraining from certain activities, or offering prayers and incense. Many Asian cultures also believe in the importance of ancestor worship, which involves honoring and remembering deceased ancestors as a way of maintaining familial connections and showing respect for previous generations.

It's important to note that Asian communities are diverse and there is a wide variety of beliefs and practices surrounding death and mourning. However, respect for the deceased and their well-being is a common theme that is seen across many Asian cultures.

Vietnamese elders want to die at home, not in the hospital or somewhere else. When a person dies, his or her body will usually be buried underground. If cremation is preferred, the family will comply. In Vietnamese culture, it is common for elders to express a preference for dying at home rather than in a hospital or other medical facility. This is because home is seen as a place of comfort and familiarity, and many elders may feel more at ease surrounded by family and loved ones.

After a person dies, it is traditional in Vietnamese culture to bury the body underground. However, if the deceased had expressed a preference for cremation, the family would typically honor this request. In Vietnamese culture, it is also common for family members and loved ones to participate in preparing the body for burial or cremation, including washing and dressing the body.

In addition, Vietnamese culture places a strong emphasis on honoring and remembering ancestors. This may involve rituals such as offering food and incense to the deceased or participating in memorial services on important anniversaries or holidays.

It's important to note that individual beliefs and practices can vary within Vietnamese culture and that not all Vietnamese people may follow these traditions. However, a preference for dying at home and honoring ancestors are important cultural values that are often seen in Vietnamese communities.

Cambodian and Lao elders want to be at home with their families when they die. However, cremation is most often preferred over burial. Ashes are sometimes kept in the family home. In Cambodian and Lao culture, it is common for elders to express a preference for dying at home surrounded by their family and loved ones. Family members and close friends may gather to offer support, prayers, and comfort during the dying process.

After death, the body is typically prepared for cremation, which is the preferred method of disposal in these cultures. Cremation is seen as a way of releasing the soul from the physical body and allowing it to move on to the next life. The ashes may be kept in an urn, which is often displayed in the family home and treated with reverence and respect.

In addition, Cambodian and Lao cultures place a strong emphasis on ancestor veneration and the importance of maintaining strong family bonds. Ancestor worship involves offering food, incense, and other offerings to honor and remember deceased loved ones. Family members may also participate in annual memorial ceremonies and other rituals to pay tribute to their ancestors and keep their memory alive.

It's important to note that individual beliefs and practices can vary within Cambodian and Lao cultures and that not all individuals may follow these traditions. However, a preference for dying at home, cremation, and ancestor veneration are important cultural values that are often seen in these communities.

H'Mong elders want to be at home and with their families when they die. Traditionally, they prefer burial. In Hmong culture, there is a strong emphasis on family and community support during end-of-life care and after death. Hmong elders typically prefer to die at home, surrounded by their loved ones. Family members and close friends will often gather to offer comfort, prayers, and support during the dying process.

After death, the Hmong traditionally prefer burial over cremation. The body is typically prepared by washing and dressing it in traditional clothing. The burial may be preceded by a funeral ceremony that includes offerings of food and other items to the deceased, as well as prayers and rituals to honor their life and memory.

It's important to note that individual beliefs and practices can vary within the Hmong community and that some Hmong may choose cremation or other forms of disposal. However, burial and the importance of family and community support during end-of-life care and after death are important cultural values that are often seen in Hmong culture.

Jewish behavior is guided by two basic principles. All laws and customs for treating the dead are meant to ensure that the body is treated with respect and dignity. Jewish faith and culture strongly support the emotional needs of the mourners and the well-being of those who survive. The burial usually takes place within 24 hours. The body is washed and someone stays with the body throughout the night.

In Jewish tradition, there is a strong emphasis on treating the body of the deceased with respect and dignity, as well as supporting the emotional needs of the mourners and surviving loved ones.

After a Jewish person passes away, the body is typically washed and dressed in simple, plain clothing. A close family member or member of the Jewish burial society (Chevra Kadisha) will perform this ritual purification, known as tahara. The body is then placed in a plain wooden casket and is not embalmed.

Jewish law and custom dictate that burial should take place as soon as possible after death, typically within 24 hours. This is to honor the dignity of the deceased and to ensure a swift return to the earth. Mourners typically sit shiva, a period of intense mourning, for seven days after the burial. During this time, friends and family members visit the mourners to offer comfort and support.

It's important to note that there is a great deal of diversity within the Jewish community and that practices may vary depending on factors such as denomination, cultural background, and personal beliefs. However, the principles of respect for the deceased and support for the living are fundamental values that are shared by many Jewish people.

Protestant American traditions tend to not want to get other family members or friends involved. You might hear them isolate their feelings in a crisis. They often try to "protect" others from knowing the truth, particularly the children. It is important to note that while some individuals within Protestant American traditions may exhibit these behaviors, it is not a universal characteristic. Different individuals within the same tradition may have different responses to death and grief. Additionally, Protestant traditions are diverse and encompass many different denominations and beliefs, so it is difficult to make generalizations about all of them. It is important to approach each individual and family with sensitivity and respect for their unique cultural and religious perspectives on death and grief.

All people regardless of their cultural background may be sensitive or reactive to those around them when a loved one dies, regardless of the circumstances surrounding the death.

Various Practices of Religious Groups Regarding Death

Here are some examples of various practices of religious groups regarding death:

1. Christianity: Christians generally believe in an afterlife, and death is seen as a transition to eternal life. Different denominations have varying beliefs about what happens after death, but most Christians believe in a judgment day where individuals are judged according to their deeds during their lifetime. Christian funeral services often include prayers, hymns, and scripture readings, and may include a eulogy or remembrance from a family member or friend.

2. Islam: Muslims believe that death is a natural part of life and that it is predetermined by Allah. The body is washed and shrouded in a simple white cloth before burial. The funeral is typically held within 24 hours of death, and the body is buried facing Mecca. Friends and family members offer condolences to the family of the deceased and recite prayers.

3. Hinduism: Hindus believe in reincarnation and that the soul continues to be reborn into different physical bodies after death. When a person dies, their body is typically cremated and the ashes are scattered in a sacred body of water. Mourning customs may vary by region, but generally include a period of mourning for the family.

4. Buddhism: Buddhists believe in reincarnation and that death is a natural part of the cycle of birth and rebirth. Funerals are typically simple and include chanting and meditation. The body is usually cremated, and the ashes are sometimes kept in a family shrine or scattered in a special location.

5. Judaism: Jewish funerals typically occur within 24 hours of death and are conducted by a rabbi. The body is washed and dressed in a simple white shroud. Friends and family members offer condolences to the family of the deceased and may recite prayers. The body is buried in a simple wooden casket without a vault so that it can decompose naturally.

These are just a few examples of the various practices of religious groups regarding death. It is important to approach each individual and family with sensitivity and respect for their unique cultural and religious perspectives on death and grief.

JUDAISM (CONSERVATIVE)

- ➢ Death occurs when respiration and circulation are irreversibly stopped and no movement is apparent.
- ➢ Extraneous talking and conversation about death are not encouraged unless initiated by the patient.
- ➢ Someone should be present when death occurs.
- ➢ The body is not left alone until buried.
- ➢ The body should be untouched for 8 to 30 minutes when death occurs.
- ➢ Medical personnel should not wash the body but may at the family's request.
- ➢ Only orthodox persons or the Jewish Burial Society should care for the body. (This can also be done by a Jewish Funeral director designated by the community.)
- ➢ Mirrors may be covered to indicate that death has occurred.
- ➢ Orthodox Jews do not approve of autopsies.
- ➢ Organ donation is acceptable to most Jews.
- ➢ Cremation is unacceptable to Conservative Orthodox Jews.

> The body should be buried as soon as possible, within one or two days.

ROMAN CATHOLIC CHRISTIANS

> Sick people are anointed with oil by a priest. The purpose of this sacrament is for healing and for strength to endure suffering.
> People are also anointed at the time of death. The term "Last Rites" is not used.
> A priest should be contacted as soon as imminent death is apparent. It can also be done as soon as possible after death has occurred.
> Religious medals, rosaries, etc. can be pinned onto the garment of the patient.
> Organ donation and autopsies are permitted.
> The nurse attending to the death of the patient should note in the care plan that the sacraments of anointing were given.

EASTERN ORTHODOX CHRISTIANS

> Last rites are obligatory
> A priest should be notified while the patient is still conscious
> Autopsies and organ donations are not encouraged
> Cremation is discouraged

OTHER CHRISTIANS

> Most denomination's view prayer and the reading of scripture important at the time of death
> Clergy may be notified if requested by the patient or family
> Family members and lay persons are encouraged to pray at the time of death
> Views on autopsies and organ donation vary, however, most would accept these practices

MUSLIMS

> Cremation is forbidden.

> Burial is within 24 to 48 hours.
> Modesty of the sick ad dressed should be preserved.
> Body should be prepared by a Muslim according to tradition.
> It is contrary to Muslim tradition to "wail." It is believed that the deceased is punished because of the family's wailing.

NATIVE AMERICANS

> Customs vary widely depending on the tribe and to the degree that the family practices.
> Some tribes have designated people who prepare the body.
> Be sensitive to touching and moving the body.
> Ask family and other staff for more information.

DRESS CODES IN HOSPITALS, NURSING HOMES, AND HOSPICES

Dress codes in hospitals, nursing homes, and hospices can vary based on the institution's policies and the role of the individual within the facility. Here are some general guidelines:

1. Scrubs: Healthcare professionals such as nurses, doctors, and other clinical staff often wear scrubs. These are specially designed clothing that is easy to clean and can help prevent the spread of infection. The color and style of scrubs may vary based on the institution, department, or rank of the healthcare worker.

2. Uniforms: Some healthcare facilities require non-clinical staff such as housekeeping, dietary, and administrative personnel to wear uniforms. These may include polo shirts, blouses, or tunics in specific colors or designs.

3. Business attire: Visitors, family members, and volunteers may be required to dress in business attire, particularly in certain areas of the hospital or nursing home. This may include collared shirts, slacks, skirts, or dresses. Wearing comfortable, closed-toe shoes is also recommended.

4. Religious attire: Patients, visitors, and staff members may need to adhere to certain dress codes based on their religious beliefs. For example, Muslim women may wear headscarves, and Sikh men may wear turbans. Facilities may have specific policies regarding religious dress codes to ensure the safety and comfort of everyone involved.

Thus, it is important to follow dress code policies in healthcare settings to maintain a professional and safe environment.

Here are some general rules that would ensure appropriate attire:

1. Clothing should be clean, neat, and well-fitting.
2. Avoid clothing that is too revealing or too casual (such as shorts or tank tops).
3. Avoid clothing with offensive language or graphics.
4. Closed-toe shoes are generally recommended to protect feet and prevent slips.
5. Avoid excessive jewelry or accessories that may pose a safety hazard or be distracting.
6. Consider the cultural and religious norms of the patient and their family when selecting attire.
7. Scrubs are appropriate attire for healthcare professionals in clinical settings.
8. White coats or other identifying apparel may be required for certain healthcare professionals.
9. Follow any specific dress codes or uniform requirements of the healthcare facility or hospice.
10. Avoid wearing strong perfumes or scents that may bother patients with respiratory issues or allergies.
    A. Do not wear tight, formfitting clothing.
    B. Do not wear low-cut necklines.
    C. Avoid T-shirts with emblems and slogans as an outer garment.
    D. No gang-related attire.
    E. Do not wear see-through or revealing clothing.
    F. No shorts.
    G. No strong lotions, Cologne, oils, etc.

For women:

    A. Dresses or skirts should fall below the knee.

B. Avoid attire that reveals underwear straps. (Some institutions ban sleeveless dresses and blouses for this reason.)

C. No strong, lotions or perfumes, oils, etc.

D. Modest make-up

Generally speaking, wear attire that is appropriate in the business world. Ordained or licensed ministers should wear civic attire.

WHEN DO VOLUNTEER CHAPLAINS WEAR BADGES?

As a Volunteer Chaplain, you will be issued an Identification Card and a Chaplains Badge. These are the property of the Chaplaincy and may be revoked if your conduct is not acceptable to the Organization. We ask that you read, review, and adhere to the rules regarding this article. They are as follows: Volunteer chaplains may wear badges or identification when they are serving in hospitals, hospices, prisons, or other institutions. The badges or identification may help identify them as part of the chaplaincy team and allow them to access restricted areas. However, the use of badges or identification may vary depending on the institution's policies and procedures. It's important for volunteer chaplains to check with the institution they are serving to determine if wearing a badge or identification is required or recommended.

i. Keep ID cards and Badges with you at all times.

ii. Present ID cards to institutions as requested.

iii. Do not hang ID cards around your neck.

iv. Wear ID Badges, if permitted by institutions where you are serving (hospitals, prisons, jails, etc.)

v. Do not wear your Badge in public places (airports, supermarkets, parties, picnics, etc.)

vi. Wear Badges at official functions where Chaplains are present.

     vii. <u>Do</u> <u>not</u> wear Badges at church unless there is a specific function involving Chaplains.

    viii. Badges can be worn during training classes, United Covenant Chaplains conferences, graduation ceremonies, etc.

If you are not sure when to wear your Badge…ASK!

Chaplains are individuals who provide spiritual and emotional support to people in various settings such as hospitals, hospices, prisons, military organizations, and universities. They are often members of a religious group, but their work is not limited to people of their own faith. Instead, they serve people of all faiths or those with no faith at all. The attributes of chaplains vary depending on their setting and the population they serve. However, there are some general attributes that most chaplains possess:

1. Empathy: Chaplains must be empathetic to be effective. They need to be able to understand and feel the emotions of others without becoming overwhelmed or losing their objectivity. Empathy is an essential trait that helps chaplains connect with patients and their families, and helps them provide emotional support during difficult times.

2. Active Listening: Chaplains must be active listeners who can provide a safe and compassionate space for people to express their thoughts and feelings. They listen without judgment or interruption and allow patients to speak at their own pace. This helps patients feel heard, respected, and understood.

3. Cultural Competence: Chaplains must be culturally competent and have a deep understanding of diverse beliefs, traditions, and values. They must be able to work with people from different cultures and religions, and respect their beliefs and practices.

4. Communication Skills: Chaplains must have excellent communication skills, both verbal and non-verbal. They need

to be able to communicate clearly, effectively, and respectfully with patients, families, and healthcare professionals. Good communication skills also help chaplains build trust and rapport with patients and their families.

5. Professionalism: Chaplains must be professional in their interactions with patients, families, and healthcare professionals. They maintain confidentiality and respect the privacy of patients and their families. They also follow ethical guidelines and codes of conduct in their work.

6. Flexibility: Chaplains must be flexible and adaptable to the changing needs of patients and their families. They may need to work long hours, work in different settings, or provide support to people with different needs. Being flexible helps chaplains adjust to different situations and provide the best possible care to patients and their families.

7. Spiritual Depth: Chaplains must have a deep understanding of spirituality and its role in people's lives. They need to be able to provide spiritual support and guidance to patients and their families, regardless of their faith or belief system. Chaplains may help people find meaning, purpose, and hope during difficult times.

8. Self-Awareness: Chaplains must be self-aware and recognize their own biases, values, and limitations. They must be able to manage their own emotions and reactions to patients' situations and provide support without judgment or personal bias.

9. Team Player: Chaplains must be able to work collaboratively with other healthcare professionals and support staff to provide holistic care to patients and their families. They must be willing to share information and collaborate with others to ensure that patients' needs are met.

10. Resilience: Chaplains must be resilient and able to cope with the emotional demands of their work. They may encounter difficult situations and challenging emotions from patients and their families. Being resilient helps chaplains maintain their emotional balance and provide support to patients and their families without becoming overwhelmed.

In conclusion, chaplains are an essential part of the healthcare team, providing emotional and spiritual support to patients and their families during difficult times. To be effective, they must possess attributes such as empathy, active listening, cultural competence, communication skills, professionalism, flexibility, spiritual depth, self-awareness, teamwork, and resilience. By embodying these attributes, chaplains can provide compassionate care to people of all faiths and backgrounds.

NOTES

www.ingramcontent.com/pod-product-compliance
Lightning Source LLC
Chambersburg PA
CBHW071936150726
47999CB00001B/224